MW00388039

To You – the butchers, the bakers, and the candlestick makers

"It takes as much energy to wish as it does to plan."

~ Eleanor Roosevelt, former US First Lady

Taking The Scary Out of Business Plans

Business plans get a bad rap. For most people, the idea of writing a business plan brings to mind hundreds of hours spent toiling away on a 50+ -page document. That's because many people believe, for some reason, that a business plan is measured by thickness. The more pages means the thicker it is which means the more likely it is to impress people, right?

Wrong! How thick your business plan is has no bearing on the success of the plan. The real point of a business plan is to help you organize all those great ideas you have so you can build the business you've always dreamed of. To put it another way, have you ever laid awake at night, too excited to sleep, because your mind is swimming with ideas and you're terrified you'll forget everything by morning? A good business plan will help you account for and judge each of those ideas independently to determine the right path to success.

Before we talk about how you create such a plan, let's tackle the top five misconceptions people have about business plans:

Business Plan Myth #1: Business Plans Are For Investors and Since I'm Not Looking For Investment Money, I Don't Need A Business Plan

In a way you're correct. It's certainly near impossible to convince an investor to give you money for your business if you don't have a business plan. But they're not the only investors to worry about. The more important reason is that the biggest investor of all shouldn't be willing to put their hard-earned time and money into this business without a plan. That investor is YOU! No matter how big or small the business you're dreaming of, you are going to be investing your time and your money to get it started. So shouldn't you take your ideas out for a test drive first? That's what a business plan can help you do.

At some point, down the road, you might decide to take your business plan to other investors as you look for additional capital to help grow your business, but at this stage in the business writing process the focus should be on creating a plan that will guide *you* in your business decisions. While the plan you're about to create can be modified into an investor-worthy presentation, the focus here is to create a plan that will help you evaluate your ideas and create a roadmap for your business.

What if I've already started my business? Is this book still for me?

Absolutely! Just because your business is already established doesn't mean you don't need a current business plan. Perhaps you initially started your business without a business plan – in that case, this book will help you build on your experiences and organize your ideas for maximum success going forward. If you already have a business plan but it hasn't been updated recently, it makes sense to revisit it now and revise it as needed. This workbook can help you do just that and make sure you don't overlook anything.

Business Plan Myth #2: Size Matters

As mentioned earlier, the final page count of your business plan doesn't have any bearing on whether or not your business will succeed. This is especially true when talking about small businesses created by solopreneurs, artisans, or craftsman like yourself. A good business plan is one that helps you collect and organize your thoughts and ideas and develop a plan of attack on how you're going to use those ideas to realize your goals. The more succinctly you can do that, the more likely you are to use your business plan as a guide and not simply file it away in a drawer.

Business Plan Myth #3: Business Plans Must Be Written

More often than not I meet entrepreneurs who don't have business plans because, in their minds, they aren't good writers. For them, writing doesn't help organize their thoughts in a linear manner and instead creates anxiety. The idea of writing a business plan then becomes such an overwhelming and burdensome task that they'd rather forgo creating a business plan altogether (and in some cases this means they abandon their entrepreneurial aspirations as well!).

If a business plan is meant to act as a guide for you, shouldn't it be created in a manner that makes sense to you? Notice that I said *created* and not *written*. We all filter information differently so if you are more of a visual learner what's stopping you from creating a visual business plan? I've seen business plans where entrepreneurs have literally drawn out sections of the plan or cut out pictures from magazines and pasted them onto a page. I've also seen entrepreneurs use Pinterest and 'pin' online images to a business planning board. If you're more technologically-driven, you could use PowerPoint or Abode Illustrator to create a combination of text, images, shapes, and graphs to help you solidify and convey your thoughts. Or maybe you want to rely on an old-fashioned pencil and paper to handwrite out your plan.

This concept of creating a 'non-written' business plan goes against the grain of traditional business planning, but in coaching and working with thousands of entrepreneurs over the years, I've personally met a fair number who used this tactic rather than relying on a written plan. Since the purpose of the business plan is to help you develop a blueprint for your business, you need to create a business plan in whichever manner makes the most sense to you; be it writing, drawing, stamping, stickering, computer animating, or any other method you're comfortable with. No matter what style of learning and creating best suits you, this workbook will walk you through the necessary steps and the questions you need to ask in order to create a solid business plan.

However, if you're creating a business plan that you'll be showing to potential investors, either friends and family, bank loan officers, or angel investors, then you should prepare a written business plan. The bank official may appreciate the creativity in your visual magazine-cutouts-on-poster board, collage-style business plan, but they're unlikely to grant you a loan!

Business Plan Myth #4: Business Plans Are Only For New Businesses

You wouldn't be the first entrepreneur who skipped over the business planning step when starting a business. But the question is what's stopping you from creating that plan now? In a perfect world you would take the time to draft out a business plan before you actually start, but it's not too late now. Take where you are today as a starting point and create the business plan from there.

And don't forget, business plans aren't just for businesses. They can also be used for new product or service launches within existing companies. If you're planning to release a new product or service to the marketplace, this business plan workbook will help you evaluate whether or not this new idea is a good use of your time, energy, and money as you work to grow your business.

Business Plan Myth #5: Business Plans Are One And Done

Creating a business plan is not just a big to-do item that you get to check off your list when it's done. A good business plan is a reference tool and will help guide your day-to-day decision making. As you run your small business, it's so easy to get mired in the everyday operations of the business that it's tough to step back and look at your business from the 10,000 foot level. Don't fall into the trap of only having time to work in your business and never being able to work on your business.

That's where the business planning process comes in. Done right, your business plan should be your constant companion throughout the upcoming year; keeping you on track towards those 10,000 foot goals. To help you do just that, at the end of this workbook you'll create a one-page Action Plan that you can stick next to your computer, on your fridge, near your workstation, or in some other prominent spot and refer to throughout the year in order to make sure that your daily business decisions are in line with your overall business plan.

Similarly, just because you create one business plan doesn't mean you never have to create another. The marketplace is ever changing, consumer behavior evolves, and so too will your business goals. You should make time to revisit your business plan at least once a year to revise it as needed and plan for the subsequent 12 months. Sometimes, to accomplish this, entrepreneurs will hole themselves up at their desk for a few hours to rework their business plan in one sitting but it's also not unheard of for entrepreneurs to 'take a break' from the real world, hand the kids over to the spouse, and check into a hotel for a day or two to work in uninterrupted silence until the new plan is complete. One entrepreneur I know spends the day after Christmas, when everyone in the house is occupied with their new books, toys, and clothes, squirrelled away in his basement reworking his business plan disruption-free.

Creating a solid plan does take time and focus whether it's your first business plan or your tenth. But just like you wouldn't get into your car without some idea of where you were going, you also shouldn't jump into a new year of business without a plan in place to help you achieve your goals.

So now that you know what a business plan is and what it isn't, let's dive in and get started.

How To Use This Workbook

This workbook is designed to take you through the questions, issues, and strategic decisions that are integral to a well-designed business plan. Following the format of traditional business plans, this workbook is divided into four main sections – Business Concept, Marketplace, Financials, and Action Plan, each with a number of related sub-sections. In the end, you will have a working business plan encapsulated within this workbook and a plan of action to move your business forward. Use this workbook at your own pace and, though many of the components build off of one another, you can skip around as needed if that's what suits you best. Remember this is not a race to the finish. This is your opportunity to carefully think through your business idea or your current business position. Whether it takes you an afternoon to get through this workbook or several months, work at your own pace so that you create a business plan that you'll be proud of and can rely on.

Throughout this workbook we will also follow the business planning process of two fictional companies. Aunt B's Jams, a small artisan jam maker, is an example of a product-based company. Drew's Dog Walking Service is an example of a services-focused company in that Drew isn't selling a tangible product, like jam, and is instead essentially billing clients for his time. These two companies are designed to help illustrate specific points within that section and completed worksheets for each company are included as a reference for you. From time to time, other fictional companies are mentioned in this workbook as well to serve as further examples.

Timeline

Most business plans for start-up businesses look out 3-5 years in order to determine whether or not the business will be profitable within that timeframe. Additionally, those businesses also create annual business plans that help to ensure that the goals they're working towards this year are moving them towards those longer-range goals as outlined in their longer-range business plan. This workbook can be used for either timeline – be it a longer range 3-5 years out or the more immediate 12 months. Simply adjust or add to the worksheets in each section as needed to lengthen or shorten the time horizon.

Creating A Space To Work

It can be hard, if not impossible, to find concentrated time to work on your business plan. If you find yourself in this position, before you sit down with this workbook here are a few tips to help you:

1. Start with a clean slate: Do you have trouble finding your desk under the piles of paper? Or perhaps your desk doubles as the dining room table and your invoices or business licensing paperwork is mixed in with your kids' art projects and report cards. This is a

great time to spend a day organizing yourself, your piles, and your workspace so that everything is clean, tidy, and properly filed. This will make it easier for you to find vital documents and will help you be more efficient going forward. Plus, speaking from experience, you might find that 'gem of an idea' you wrote down six months ago and then promptly forgot as you start tackling that paper pile on your desk.

2. Streamline Online: If your email inbox is inundated with daily newsletters, sales requests, and discount deals, go through it and unsubscribe to any email correspondence that's just clogging up your inbox. While you're at it, delete all those old messages you no longer need or file away into e-folders those that you want to hold onto for future reference.

3. Find 90: It's hard to really get into working on your plan if all you have are bits and pieces of time where your focus is constantly being diverted. If it's hard to find significant chunks of time to work on your plan, break it down in smaller 90 minute-focused timeslots by working through one or two sub-sections of this workbook at a time. Schedule those 90 minutes in advance with yourself and guard that time – the errands, phone calls, and emails can wait. When it's your 90 minutes to work on your plan, turn off all distractions, set a timer, and dive in. When the time is up stop where you are and return to the rest of your life. The benefit of working into 90-minute slots is that it will allow you to really focus on one or two aspects of the plan rather than rushing to try and get through everything all at once. If you're pressed for time, working through the workbook in this manner will help you balance a thoughtful approach to your business plan with all those other things in your life that are vying for your attention.

SECTION 1: THE BUSINESS CONCEPT

Forget The Business Plan – Start With Your Vision

One thing top business schools are experts in is teaching students how to create a solid business plan that you can take to investors. They'll teach you about the various components that need to be in the plan and all that financial calculations you must showcase. But is that really the best place to start?

For small businesses where it's just you or maybe a partner or handful of employees working on the business, jumping right into the business plan often isn't the best first step. Instead, the initial focus should be on determining your Vision for the company. Or, to put it another way, you want to have a clear and concise understanding of what it is you want to create business-wise and how this business will affect the rest of your life before diving into the actual business planning process.

What Is Visioning?

Most typically defined as developing a clear sense of purpose, Visioning enables you to determine what you want your business and your life to look like in the future. Why are you spending the time, energy, and money to start and grow this business? If your answer is limited to financial reasons like *"So I can make millions of dollars and buy an island,"* I'd suggest taking a step back for a moment. The specific financial numbers and sales growth figures will come later in the planning process – for this exercise we're concerned less with actual numbers and are looking instead to determine how you want this business to impact you and your life. Try thinking of the Visioning from the standpoint of answering this question - what will an ideal day in your life look like several years from now?

For most entrepreneurs, financials are an important component of starting a business but how else will the business change your life? By taking a high-level look you may realize that you want a business that gives you the flexibility to stay home with your kids during summer vacations. Or perhaps you're looking to build a side business that will keep you creatively challenged while you continue to work in your somewhat-boring-but-benefits-providing full-time position elsewhere. Perhaps you want to start your business part-time now but hope to transition to full-time down the road. Everyone's needs and lifestyles are different so each person should be honest with themselves about what will make them happy both personally and professionally. Otherwise you'll quickly suck the joy out of this entrepreneurial venture.

Spend some time thinking through the answers to the following questions based on a five-year timeframe. How would that perfect day in your life look five years from today?

Visioning Worksheet

1. What time do you wake up and what does your morning rountine look like?

2. Do you work from your home, an outside-of-the-home office, a coffee shop, or do you have a workspace or, for food businesses, a commercial kitchen that is the hub of your business? Describe what this space looks like. Do you own it or rent it? Do you feel frenzied and worried when you're there or excited about the opportunities before you? Is your email in-box crammed with messages and orders? Do you have employees who will be helping you (if so, what time do you see them coming into the office/workspace).

3. What does your workday look like? Do you see yourself designing new products/taking sales calls/working on marketing material/meeting with your employees/or a combination of all of those and more? What tasks are you good at? What weaknesses have you strengthened through courses, books, or life experiences? What responsibilities have you outsourced to experts or have you hired on your own experts to be on your staff? If you're working on this business part-time describe what your work day looks like after you're done with your regular job.

4. What does your business look like at this point? Are you selling your products wholesale and, if so, how any stores are your products in? Do you have a loyal group of online customers who make up the bulk of your revenue? Do you see yourself sending off samples of your product to magazines and bloggers to review? Or perhaps your company was recently featured in your favorite media outlet? Are you planning to introduce a new product soon? What do customers think of your branding and marketing?

Visioning Worksheet

5. How long is your workday? Do you see yourself working 9 – 5? More? Less? Maybe you're a morning person and you'd like to start your day at 5 a.m.? Or maybe you have kids who need to be picked up from school so you see yourself being done by 3 p.m. every day. Perhaps your workday hours will be more sporadic because of your current life situation. There's no wrong answer, just highlight how this business fits into the life you want for yourself.

6. If there are financial goals you want your business to hit, what are they? This can be highlighted via a specific number, a monthly salary figure, or even an item that you'd buy or statues that you'd achieve (such as a frequent flyer statues) that, to you, symbolizes that you've hit your financial goals.

7. When you leave work for the day what do you do? Are you headed out for a run with your dogs or out for drinks with friends? Do you check email throughout the night or after the kids are in bed or do you shut down your computer entirely at the end of the day and into check back until the next morning? Remember, don't say that you're willing to work 24x7 if it's only going to make you miserable. Be truthful with yourself about what you want so that you can craft a business plan that will help you achieve that.

Using the following pages, your answers together into one cohesive vision. Feel free to use written words and/or images to help you convey your thoughts. Also feel free to make additional copies of the following page if one page is not enough.

Visioning Worksheet

Now, as you review your Visioning document, ask yourself what your life would look like one year from today as you work towards that five year vision of your life. Are there any short term sacrifices or changes you might need to and are willing to make in order to build this business into what you want it to be? If so, what are they?

Identifying Your Business Goals

We most often associate goals with the resolutions we all make on January 1st and vow to stick with (if you belong to a gym you know it's darn near impossible to find a free treadmill in early January!). You should approach your business similarly and spend some time thinking about what exactly you want your business to achieve in the next 12 months. Unlike the eager new gym goers who tend to disappear by mid-February though, we want your business goals to have more staying power and keep you focused and on-task all year and that's what the business plan will help you do.

The S.M.A.R.T. framework for goal setting was first introduced by George Doren in a paper written for Management Review in 1981 and it has become standard practice in the business world. Through a series of five steps, highlighted by the S.M.A.R.T. mnemonic, this framework enables business owners to crate specific goals around which all business decisions should be made.

Directions on how to fill out the following S.M.A.R.T. template:

1. *S = Specific.* As you look at the Vision Statement you created, think about and list all of the goals or milestones you want your business to hit in the next year as you work towards that longer-range vision you outlined in the last section. Using the following template, list out your goals under S = Specific. Because we're not yet concerned about focusing on a specific number of goals, write down all the goal ideas you have – feel free to make additional copies of this worksheet if need be.

   As you work through this exercise, focus on your business goals and not your personal goals as well. Potential goals might include increasing sales, winning industry awards, getting into a certain number of new stores or farmers' markets, or building a stronger business network.

2. *M = Measurable.* How are you going to know whether or not your goal has been achieved unless you can tie it to a measurable result. In the M = Measurable column revisit each of the corresponding goals and add in a benchmark or other criteria that you will use to gauge whether or not you successfully completed that goal a year from now. Using the examples from earlier, this might translate into 'Increase sales by 40%,' 'Win Cheesemaker of the year award in your local magazine,' 'Open up 15 new customer accounts,' or 'Reach 2500 Facebook fans.'

   Don't yet worry about how you're going to achieve those goals. The strategies you employ are what you develop in your marketing plan. For now we're trying to determine which goals you'll focus on for the next 12 months. If there are goals you originally outlined that can't be measured then drop them from your list and focus instead on the measurable ones going forward through the next steps.

3. *A = Attainable.* It's admirable to have lofty goals, but in business you want to focus on the goals that you can actually reasonably achieve. So now it's time to ask whether the goals are attainable in the next 12 months. In some cases, your goals may be more like a wish list – for example, 'Get mentioned in 5 major magazines' holiday gift lists' but there's a significant amount of luck involved with that goal that's out of your control. Similarly, you may have goals that you're simply not in the position to achieve right now. For example, you may want to increase sales by 40% but if you don't have the ability to increase production or don't have the time available to service additional clients, then that goal is not attainable at this time.

   Revisit your Specific, Measurable Goals and assess whether or not they are attainable. In some cases a goal may need to be revised to become attainable while other goals may prove to be unrealistic right now. After you make any revisions necessary, continue onto Step 4 with a focus on only those goals that you believe are attainable.

4. *R = Relevant.* Do the remaining goals make sense for your business and are they focused in such a way that you believe they will move the needle for you? For example, 'Increasing your Facebook Fan Base to 2500' is a great goal but if you don't think your

target market is very social-media savvy then that goal is not relevant to your business. Think about your business and the goals you've outlined and write 'Yes' or 'No' next to each one in the R = Relevant column. You only want to focus on those that you deem relevant moving forward.

5. *T = Time Frame.* What sort of timeline are you giving yourself to achieve these goals? Are they goals that will take a good chunk of the coming year to achieve? Or do you have goals listed that you expect to be completed sooner?

You don't want to build your business plan around short-term goals that can be accomplished fairly quickly but by the same token you also don't want to focus on goals that will take you more than a year to complete. In the later case, it's better to break those long-range goals into smaller 12-month goals that you can work towards. In the T = Time Frame column indicate what deadlines or targets you're shooting for with each goal.

S.M.A.R.T. Goal Setting

S=Specific M=Measurable A=Attainable R=Relevant T=Timeframe

S.M.A.R.T. Goal Setting
(Aunt B's Jams)

S=Specific   M=Measurable   A=Attainable   R=Relevant   T=Timeframe

Increase sales	Increase monthly sales by 36%	yes	yes	12 months
Add new flavor profiles	Introduce 3 new flavors in this year	yes	yes	12 months
Improve product pictures	Have all products professionally photographed	No - don't have the money for this at this time		
Open up wholesale accounts	Get into 5 retail locations	yes	yes	12 months
Start an artisan peanut butter-and-jam festival	Get over 20 vendors & 1000 visitors	No - don't have the time to organize an event of this scale		
Start a jam of the month direct-to-consumer delivery service	Attain 2500 new jam-of-the-month customers	yes	yes	36 months

S.M.A.R.T. Goal Setting
(Drew's Dog Walking)
S=Specific M=Measurable A=Attainable   R=Relevant T=Timeframe

Add more customers	10 more regular weekly customers	yes	yes	12 months
Sell dog food & treats to my clients	Sell $400 worth of food & treats to my clients	No - don't have the cash to buy in food & treat inventory		
Increase services to include dog training classes	Provide 6-week dog socialization training	yes	yes	9 months
Ease client's scheduling concerns	Reduce client email volume & phone calls checing in to see if their dog is on this week's schedule	Yes - create personalized online calendar that clients can log-in to view	yes	4 months
Franchise Drew's Dog Walking Company	Open 4 new franchise locations	No - dog walking services are easily copied, not sure there's market need for franchise		
Reduce accidents to dogs & walkers	One year without any accidents	yes	yes	12 months

Picking Your Top Three

As a small business entrepreneur, most likely with a very limited staff (if any staff at all!), you want to limit your focus to your top three S.M.A.R.T. goals. It's very difficult with all the other business (and personal) needs you have fighting for your attention daily to also work towards accomplishing a laundry list of goals without spreading yourself too thin. The goals that stand the best chance of helping you drive your business forward are those in which all five S.M.A.R.T. steps could be completed. Of those, determine which three are the most important to you and to your business.

Go back now and determine which three goals are going to guide your business strategy in the next 12 months. Using the following worksheet, write down your top three goals. Examples of Aunt B's Jams and Drew's Dog Walking Service's main goals are also shown on following pages.

Top Three Business Goals

S=Specific   M=Measurable A=Attainable   R=Relevant   T=Timeframe

Top Three Business Goals
(Aunt B's Jams)

S=Specific   M=Measurable A=Attainable   R=Relevant   T=Timeframe

Increase Jam Sales	Increase monthly sales by 36%	yes	yes	12 months
Add new flavor profiles	Introduce 3 new flavors in the year	yes	yes	12 months
Open up wholesale accounts	Get into 5 retail locations	yes	yes	12 months

Top Three Business Goals
(Drew's Dog Walking Services)
S=Specific   M=Measurable   A=Attainable   R=Relevant   T=Timeframe

Gain more customers	Gain 10 more regular weekly customers	yes	yes	12 months
Ease client's scheduling concerns	Reduce client email volume & phone calls checking in to see if their dog is on this week's schedule	Yes - create personalized online calendar that clients can login to view	yes	4 months
Reduce accidents & injuries to dogs and walkers	One year without any accidents or injuries	yes	yes	12 months

What's Your BHAG?

The term BHAG – which stands for BIG HAIRY AUDATIOUS GOAL – was coined by Jim Collins and Jerry Porras in their classic business book *Built To Last*. A BGAH is a long-range goal that succinctly sums up information from your vision statement to create an overarching ambition for you business that all other goals and decisions are built upon. One of the most famous examples is John F. Kennedy's BHAG which was to have a man on the moon by the end of the 1960's. You may not be looking to walk on the moon but that doesn't mean you shouldn't shoot for it. Small Food Business' (the business I founded and currently run) is to be the most trusted source of business information for artisan food entrepreneurs. That's no small task but a good BHAG should be something that will inspire you (and any employees you have or may have in the future) every single day. So what's your purpose? What's your BHAG?

Business Overview

Based on the work you've completed thus far, you're now ready to create your company overview. In no more than a paragraph, explain what your business is including what you plan to sell and why and what goals you hope to achieve. This should be a short company description so that anyone could, from this one paragraph, understand what it is your company does.

This short overview also serves as a starting point for your marketing material, for future press releases, and even for you when asked by someone what you do for a living. This overview is also the first part of any business plan that potential investors want to see so that they understand what it is you're trying to accomplish. Over time your business overview may change and become more refined, so don't worry if it doesn't necessarily feel perfect today.

Company Description

_____

_____

_____

_____

_____

Company Description
(Aunt B's Jams)

Aunt B's Jams is a jam and spread company that handcrafts traditional flavors using locally-sourced ingredients from recipes that have been handed-down for generations. While the focus is on authentic flavors, Aunt B's does try to take a modern spin on these recipes.

Company Description
(Drew's Dog Walking Service)

Drew's Dog Walking Service is a pet services company that focuses on providing active breeds with excercise and an outlet for their energy by offering 1-hour walks.

Say It Out Loud

As mentioned earlier, your business overview is the basis of your elevator pitch – the quick summation of what your business does that should take no longer than a quick elevator ride to explain to a stranger. The idea behind the elevator pitch is imagining that you step into an elevator and there, before you, is someone who could really help your business. Perhaps it's the publisher of a magazine you'd love to get your product into, maybe it's a buyer or owner of a retail store you're hoping to get your product sold in, or it could be a client you've been trying to land for months – no matter who it is, you need to be able to clearly and succinctly explain your business to them in a manner that makes them eager to know more. What sort of impression do you think you'll make it you stumble over your words or struggle to find the right way to explain what you do? While you may believe wholeheartedly in your company and what you're trying to create, that enthusiasm doesn't always come through when we feel like we're put on the spot – especially if you're not a born salesperson. So practice saying your Business Overview out loud. You may need to change some words in order to make it sound more natural when spoken, but by practicing your Business Overview, the better chance you have of making sure your excitement and belief in your products or services comes across clearly and confidently when explaining to others what you do.

Understanding Your Strengths And Weaknesses

Thus far you've outlined what it is you want your business to be, what you're working towards achieving, and how this business will fit into your life, but no business is perfect so we need to take some time to understand what strengths and weaknesses your business has as well as what threats and opportunities it faces. A SWOT Matrix (where S stands for Strength, W for Weakness, O for Opportunities, and T for Threats) is a great exercise to guide you as you think through these aspects of your business. Traditionally laid out in a square that is divided into four quadrants, the idea behind the SWOT Matrix is that you fill each section with the strengths, weaknesses, opportunities, and threats your business faces.

If you've already started your business, this process may be fairly easy to walk through based on your experiences thus far. If, however, you haven't yet started your business, don't feel like you won't be able to complete this section. The SWOT matrix will help you identify those aspects within your proposed business model. Simply use the questions provided to help you think through the SWOT Matrix to help identify different strengths, weakness, threats, and opportunities in your proposed business model.

If you have any staff or business partners they can assist with this process but advisors, family members, or friends may be able to also point out aspects of your business that fall into one of these categories that you've forgotten or simply overlooked. The more feedback you can get the better you can identify positives and negatives in your business and then work towards either capitalizing on them or steps to nullify them.

Ask yourself the following questions as you fill out a SWOT Matrix for your business:

Strength Quadrant

In this section you want to list out those parts of your business that are well-suited to help the business succeed so look at things like:

- What does your company do well or what do you believe it will excel at? What products are/will be well-received and why? Are your products specialized in a way that the target market cares about?

- What skills, expertise, or connections do you, your staff/contractors, or advisors have that sets you up for success. This might include a trusted bookkeeper who's a genius with numbers, a graphic designer who 'gets' your vision, or even your own sales skills that makes you fearless when talking with buyers.

- What is/what do you think will be your best-selling product or service? What is/will be your highest profit margin product or service? They're not always the same thing!

- What do you or will you do better than your competitors?

Weakness Quadrant

Here you want to look for things that may hinder your business growth such as:

- Take a look at your own skills and the skills of any staff or partners you may have, what business functions could use more attention and focus (hint – they're usually the tasks that you dread doing!)? What skills might you and your team be lacking?

- For product businesses, are there any parts of your product production and packaging that are a bigger-than-expected time or money drain? Alternatively, do you believe any of your product production and/or packaging will be a drain on resources?

- Do you have enough money to help finance your business in a way that will make it possible for you to achieve the goals you've laid out for the next 12 months?

- Are there resources, equipment, etc. that you are lacking?

- Are there areas of your business that cost you too much money? One common complaint by products businesses is that they aren't able to negotiate competitive prices for their raw materials because they aren't producing quantities at a level that provides them with price discounts for those materials.

- Are there other logistical challenges you face such as production capacity, storage, transportation of goods, shelf life, etc.? For services businesses this might include things like an office or professional workspace to hold meetings in.

- Are any of your products or services slower sellers or not giving you a healthy profit margin or do you foresee potential slow sellers among your proposed product or services line?

Opportunities Quadrant

In this section you want to outline those aspects of your business that are well situated to grow or could help you further solidify a loyal customer base. For example:

- What else can you do for your target customers? This might be new product development, it might be enhanced customer service, it might be new technology like a new website that makes the client's meeting scheduling experience more streamlined.

- Are there new target markets that you could try to reach out to?

- Are there trends or changes in the marketplace that you've identified that you can take advantage of?

- Are there potential strategic partnerships with other businesses that you might be able to leverage?

- Are there any funding sources that you might be able to approach for more money (such as grants, SBA loans, etc.) or experts you can collaborate with to help you grow your business?

Threats Quadrant

In this area we want to take a look at what external forces might slow or hinder your business growth. Consider the following:

- What are your competitors' greatest strengths? What are they doing well that you're not able to because of lack of staff, funding, time, resources, etc.?

- Are there trends or changes in the marketplace that you've identified that may hamper your business growth? As an example, a recession or economic downturn can make selling high-priced items more difficult so if you produce a luxury product or provide a luxury service this would be a concern and should be added to this quadrant.

- Do you foresee changes in your industry or is there any proposed legislation that may impact your business?

- Are there specific obstacles your business faces that cannot be easily remedied? For example, perhaps you have a ten-year lease on a building that is not in the best location.

SWOT Matrix

Strengths	**Weaknesses**
Opportunities	**Threats**

SWOT Matrix
(Aunt B's Jams)

Strengths

- Use locally-saved fruits from family-owned small farms in all jams
- Craft extraordinarily good jam based on traditional recipes
- I'm a passionate salesperson – love to tell my story & the story of my jams
- Strawberry jam is the top seller

Weaknesses

- Raw ingredients are more expensive resulting in an expensive end product
- Recipes are basic flavors like strawberry, raspberry, blackberry, etc. Not differentiated.
- Amount of jam I can produce is highly dependent on how the local weather impacts fruit harvests
- Blackberry jam provides a very low profit margin because blackberries are so costly
- Packaging was designed on my home computer and look amateur. May impact how the brand is perceived.

Opportunities

- Enhanced packaging
- Build an online e-commerce store so that people can order online
- Branch out into more unique flavor combinations
- Potential to work with area restaurants and bakeries that may use jam in their products, but don't want to have to make their jam from scratch
- Create a low-sugar line specifically for children and diabetics

Threats

- Popularity in canning means more people than ever are making jams at home
- Numerous small jam producers make the market place very competative
- Low cost to start a jam company means more competitors enter the marketplace everyday
- Big jam brands are running ads trying to convince customers that their jams are "handmade" and less expensive

SWOT Matrix
(Drew's Dog Walking Service)

Strengths

- I get along great with dogs
- Young "two-income-no-kids" people in this city work long hours but want the best for their dog(s)

Weaknesses

- The time it takes to drive around to the different neighborhoods & pick up all the dogs keeps me from being able to walk even more dogs
- Not all dogs get along with other dogs so some dogs can only be walked solo and not in groups
- Hard for clients to reach during the day because I'm out walking the dogs and unable to answer my phone

Opportunities

- Dog population is growing in this area
- Expand to other neighborhoods within the area
- Add dog-running outings options for high-energy breeds for whom a walk is not enough

Threats

- Rising gas prices eat significantly into my profits
- Risk of lawsuit or bad recommendations if a dog gets injured or gets into a fight
- If local economy falters more people will stay home and not need dog walking services

Using The SWOT Matrix

Once you've filled in all the sections of the SWOT, you want to use the information to help you recognize strategies that can help you achieve your business goals. Using your SWOT Matrix as a guide, consider the following as you work through the rest of this workbook to create your business plan:

• See if there are any strengths that you might want to build upon because they will provide substantial movement towards your business goals. Can you use any of your strengths to knock out any of the threats you identified?

• Assess your weaknesses and determine which ones you can begin to shore up.

• Determine whether any of the opportunities you've outlined are worth going after and, if so, create goals on how you're going to achieve that. Based on the strengths you outlined, can any of those help you more quickly leverage an opportunity? Similarly, if any of the opportunities would require something that is a weakness of yours in order to be achieved, it may be worthwhile exploring how quickly that weakness can be strengthened so that you can take advantage of this opportunity.

• Develop plans that will help you combat the threats your business faces.

Much like a business plan, a SWOT Matrix shouldn't be something you only do once and never look at again. Because market conditions are constantly changing, as is your business, it's a tool that you should revisit at least once a year as it can help guide your decision-making for the following year.

Rules & Regulations

Depending on what type of business you envision, there may be certain city, state, or even federal regulations you have to meet before your business is allowed to legally operate; including but not limited to obtaining your business license and permits. For our jam company, Aunt B's needs to get her county health permit before she's able to sell her products. Businesses like esthetician services, daycares, etc. all need special licenses to operate. Even if your business doesn't fall into this category, there may be safety training or critical business skills you feel are important to brush up on before starting your business. For example, in the case of our dog walker, he decided that it was important to take a Pet First Aid & CPR course. On the following few lines, write down any mandated licensing your business needs as well as training you deem critical. This will act as a reminder that we'll later add to your short-term task list after you've completed the business plan.

Rules & Regulations

_____

_____

_____

_____

_____

Rules & Regulations
(Aunt B's Jams)

- County health permit required
- Food handler's certificate needed

_____

_____

_____

Rules & Regulations
(Drew's Dog Walking Service)

- Take pet first aid + CPR course
- Become a member of City Dog Walkers Association

If you've completed all sections thus far, you now have a solid foundation for your business plan. No matter how strong your business model is though, your business doesn't operate in a vacuum. In order to be successful you need to have a thorough understanding of the marketplace you're entering which includes understanding who your customers are, who your competitors are, and how you're going to position your company. We'll focus on this in the next section.

Section Checklist

- Complete Vision Plan

- Outline Short Term Sacrifices

- Identify S.M.A.R.T. Goals

- Narrow to Top 3 Goals

- Determine What Your BHAG Is

- Write and Practice Saying Your Company Description

- Identify Strengths, Weaknesses, Opportunities, and Threats

- Obtain Required Business Licenses and Permits and Complete Any Necessary Training

SECTION 2: THE MARKETPLACE

The Marketplace section of a business plan is the foundation of your marketing plan. What we'll learn by working through this section will serve as the basis for all marketing and branding decisions you make as well as help direct your overall business strategy.

Understanding Who Your Target Market Is And How To Find Them

It's not uncommon, when talking to a small business entrepreneur, that when asked who their target market is they look surprised. "Target market," they say, "everyone loves my product!"

Unfortunately 'everyone' is a gross overgeneralization regardless of what type of business you have. You simply can't have a product or service that will appeal to everyone. Even giant companies don't try to appeal to everyone all at once. Companies like Gap, Inc., for example, also own multiple brands including Gap, Banana Republic, Old Navy, Piperlime, and Athleta, because they know that not everyone is the same and what an athletic 40-year-old wants in a pair jeans is likely very different from what a trendy 13-year-old wants. The big brands understand that even with all of their marketing power they can't convince 'everyone' to buy the same product so they create different products and brands that are marketed to different groups of people. Those companies understand that each target market has different needs and different buying behaviors.

As a small business owner, you should follow suit and focus on understanding what types of people would most likely purchase your product or service. Your goal is to understand everything you can about this group of people; about how they make their buying decisions, where they shop, and what their needs or concerns are. You want to be able to determine whether they'd be more likely to buy your product at a store or at a craft fair or farmers' market or whether they'd be more likely to research your company online or ask friends for recommendations before hiring you for their services needs. Knowing what is important to these consumers is at the core of every successful business strategy no matter how big or small the business.

The big-brands have entire research departments and huge budgets focused on knowing everything they can about their target market. They can break their customers down into segmented groups such as Power Shopper, Social-Media Mom, and After-work Coach Dad. You can do the same thing for your business – albeit on a smaller scale. Not only will this help give you a better return on investment on your company's marketing and advertising, but it will also help answer that critical question of how much you should charge since the more you know about your ideal customers the more you understand how much money they're willing to pay for your company's products or services.

So how do you do this on your limited small business budget? The first thing that you need to understand, at a high level, is why someone would buy your products or hire your company. Researchers have discovered that people make buying decisions for one of three reasons:

Why People Buy

1 To satisfy a basic need

2 To solve problems

3 To make themselves feel good

As you think about the products or services your company will offer, does one of the above reasons jump out at you? Most people assume that services companies fall into the second category but it's not quite that simple. Taking our dog-walking service example, not only does this company solve a problem for the customer by offering the dog an active outlet during the day, but it also helps the customer feel good that his/her dog is being taken care of and having fun even when the customer is at work. Essentially, Drew's Dog Walking Service makes the customer feel less guilty about leaving their dog at home alone all day.

Products-based companies can fall into any of the three categories above. Taking a look at our fictional Aunt B's Jams company, to peanut-butter and jelly sandwich lovers, the jam could actually be considered a basic need but it also makes the customers feel good about what they're eating because they're choosing a locally-crafted jam over a mass manufactured product. Already you can start to see market segments emerge. Since it may be hard to identify who the toast and pb& j-lovers are (unless you found a blog pb&j blog), it makes sense to focus on people who love jam but who are looking for a healthier alternative to big brand jams.

Fill out the following with what you know about your customers or potential customers. Remember, you may not be able to answer every question.

Find Your Target Market

What basic need does your product or service fill? _____

_____

_____

_____

_____

_____

What problem does your product or service solve? _____

_____

_____

_____

_____

_____

How do customers feel when they buy your product or service?

_____

_____

_____

_____

_____

Consumer Psychology 101: The Emotional Reasons People Buy

Experts have found that people not only make purchasing decisions based on the rational reasons they're presented with – i.e., this product has fruit and grains and is therefore healthy – but there is also an emotional driver that plays a large role in why people buy what they buy and why they choose the brands or companies that they do. As an example, someone may buy that chocolate chip cookie because they've had a rough day and they feel they deserve it. The key word in that sentence is 'feel' – there is an emotional reason behind why they're spending money on a product or service and it may have nothing to do with the actual attributes of that product or service.

The 12 emotions or motivations that experts have identified consumers are looking to fill when making a purchase are:

- Accomplished
- Adventurous
- Connected
- Creative
- Transformed
- Important
- Playful
- Wise
- Youthful
- Sensual
- Rebellious
- Responsible

If you think that people buy a product or service and determine which emotional need it fills afterwards, it's important to note that people are not always aware of these emotional triggers. Yet they still seek out companies who will help them fill those emotional needs. To better illustrate this, let's look at the example of a bride-to-be. She is trying to determine which local bakery she wants to design her wedding cake but, like anything wedding-related, her family has their opinions too and they're not shy about sharing!

The bride's father, a rather conservative individual, is trying to get the bride to pick the local country club bakery which is known for its traditional tiered cakes. For him the cake is a status symbol that will help show guests how important and successful he is. The bride herself is angling to use the local vegan bakery even though she's not vegan herself but it's her little act of rebellion against her conservative parents. The bride's younger sister doesn't understand why everyone is looking at such boring cakes and is dropping hints that if the bride wants to let her creativity shine through she should pick the baker whose portfolio was full of colorful, topsy-turvy cakes. And then, there's the future mother-in-law who thinks the prices the bakeries charge for wedding cakes these days is an irresponsible use of money and she keeps telling her soon-to-be daughter-in-law that they should save their money and just order a cake from Costco instead and be done with it.

As you can see, every single person involved with that purchasing decision has a different motivation for why they want to work with a certain bakery. You'll notice that in this example not one of the reasons mentioned had anything to do with the actual flavor or consistency of the cake – the actual product attributes – but instead had to do with each individual's personal feelings and emotions.

What emotions do your products satisfy for customers? Remember, you have to look at this through the lens of your target market and take into consideration what you know about them. Rank these in the order of importance, putting N/A for any emotions you believe aren't relevant to your customers' purchasing decisions.

Customer Emotions Worksheet

Rank the emotions your target customers might feel when purchasing your product or service. *(Leave blank those that don't apply.)*

_____ Accomplished

_____ Adventurous

_____ Connected

_____ Creative

_____ Important

_____ Transformed

_____ Playful

_____ Wise

_____ Youthful

_____ Sensual

_____ Rebellious

_____ Responsible

Who Are These Customers?

Now that you're starting to think about the motivations behind why someone would buy your product or service, you also want to learn more about the people themselves and see if any demographic patterns emerge. If you're planning to sell your products locally (at least at first) or offer a service that is only available to a local market, you can find a lot of demographic information about the people in your area for free via the US Census report which is available online at www.census.gov. You should also try contacting your library and Chamber of Commerce to see what information and research they might have access to. If you're already selling your products or services, you can also tap into what you already know about your customers' preferences and behavior. For any questions where you don't have information or data, you can always try talking informally to a few potential customers or, as a last resort, go with your gut feeling.

Target Market Demographic Questions

- What type of person is buying/will buy your products or services? Describe what a typical day in their life is like.
- What is their age range?
- Are they married or single?
- Do they have children and, if so, what is the age range of their children?
- What is their average annual income?
- Briefly describe what a typical day in your target market's day might be like. Are they crunched for time because of work and family commitments? Are they stressed out college kids?
- Why would they buy your products or services – to satisfy a need, solve a problem, or to make themselves feel good? You can take this a step further by asking yourself what need their fulfilling, problem solving, or emotion they're feeling. For example, do you envision beautiful packaging of your product in which case someone may buy your product to give as a gift to someone else. Or maybe you're offering maternity photo sessions in which case someone may buy a session with you in order to help them capture their pregnancy on film. Be as specific as possible.
- How do they feel about your price points (this one really is best answered by talking to potential customers or, at worst, friends and family, for feedback)?

Now, based on your answers to the Target Market demographic questions, you can write a description of who your ideal customer is. For Aunt B's Jams, this might read:

'My target customer is a 30-40-year-old mom who takes pride in feeding her family handcrafted products that are made with ingredients she trusts.'

With this knowledge Aunt B can start to develop a distribution strategy (perhaps farmers' markets where Aunt B can interact and share her story with customers), determine the right pricing (since these moms are more likely to pay more for organic, the jams can be priced above mass-produced everyday jams), and can determine which products would appeal to that market (strawberry, raspberry, and orange marmalade ought to be well received whereas kumquat may be a bit too exotic to make kids happy). This information also shows that Aunt B's Jams is a good name for her business since her target market values a human connection with the food they buy.

It's impossible to be everything to everyone – especially for a small business with a limited budget. But by identifying your target market and learning what you can about them, you'll be on the road to becoming the go-to company for a group of people who value what you offer.

Based on your research and intuition and the questions you answered in the Target Market Demographic Questions Worksheet, write a one or two sentence customer description.

Customer Description
(Aunt B's Jams)

My target customer is a 30-40-something mom who takes pride in feeding her family handcrafted products that are made with ingredients she trusts.

My target customer is a mid 20-mid 30 working professional who doesn't have children but who thinks of their dog as their child. They feel guilty leaving their dog crated all day while they work and want the dog to have exercise and mental stimulation.

The Competitive Landscape

We've spent a lot of time thus far learning more about you, your company, and your target market. But, like all businesses, you don't operate in a vacuum so it's now time to understand who your competitors are. No matter how 'new' or 'handcrafted,' your products are, consumers have a limited amount of disposable income that they're willing to spend and you need to understand how your company stacks up against your competitors. This information will help you make strategic marketing decisions as well as convey to customers what makes your products or services different from all the rest.

Where Do You Fit?

The first step in the competitive analysis is to determine where you fit within your industry and within the market you serve. No matter how unique your product or company is, if you can't succinctly describe what it is you then you'll have a hard time explaining to customers why they need your products or services. Perhaps you've created a new iPhone app for children – in this case you are operating in the 'children,' 'education,' and 'technology' space. Customers need to understand where you fit in the overall product or services landscape, what it is you're selling, and how you're different.

For example, our dog walker Drew might choose the category of *pet care* to describe his services whereas the jam company would say that it is *artisan food*, and *jams and jellies*.

Pick no more than 3 or 4 words to describe what categories your products or services fall into.

Company Categories
(Aunt B's Jams)

* Specialty food, artisan food
* Jams, jellies, spreads

Company Categories
(Drew's Dog Walking Service)

* Pet care services
* Dog care

You need to know everything you can about all of your competitors within your category and the following Competitor Evaluation worksheet is designed to help you do just that. To fill out the worksheet, first identify who you perceive to be your closest competitors. Keep in mind that you don't need to do this for every competitor out there. Focus on those companies who directly compete with you for the same or similar target audiences within the same category and within the same target area. For example, if you've identified that your target market for your children's iPhone app is moms who want to help their children excel at reading, then you would want to highlight other apps that promise the same results as well as in-person educational facilities and reading programs like Reading With Rover where libraries and schools bring in trained dogs who the children read to in order to practice their reading skills. Aunt B's Jams would look at other local competitors who sell in her area and not worry too much about the national brands as they attract a different target market than who she's going after and Drew, our dog walker, isn't going to worry too much about cat walkers (is there such a thing?!) but will include other dog walking services who service the same metro area.

After you've identified who your major competitors are, you should indicate what products or services they offer that are similar or identical to what you have. This is also a great time to make note of other products or services they offer and ask yourself if those are products or services your target customers may also want. You don't necessarily need to change business strategy based on this information, but it's good to know what your competitors are doing as it enables you to change course quickly and modify your plans if you find that's what the market demands.

In the third column of the worksheet, you can either put in the company's average price point or indicate the range within which the competitor prices their products and services. This will be information you refer back to later when you start pricing your products or services.

Marketing Attributes are those things that the competitor identifies as being different or unique about their product or services. Perhaps they are saying that their product offers health or education benefits (like the iPhone reading app), maybe they're saying that their jams are lower in sugar than regular jams, or maybe they're saying that they're a certified pet psychic and so they understand what dogs are thinking and feeling during walks. Whatever the case may be, it's important that you understand how your competitors are trying to differentiate themselves to consumers.

In the Target Market column you should put, based on your best guess, who the target market is for that competitor. For example, the low sugar jam competitor is likely marketing itself to diabetics and those trying to lose weight. The Perceived Strengths and Perceived Weaknesses columns are also where you're going to input, based on what you can find out about your competitors, how the company compares to yours – what do they do better and what do you do better? It's hard to be impartial when it comes to this section so this might be a great time to rope in a friend or family member and get their opinion.

Competitors' websites and social media channels can provide you with a wealth of competitive information. Take a look at their sites to see how the company is being positioned, what sort of claims they're making, and to see pictures of their products and packaging as applicable. All of this is valuable information that can help you learn more about your competitors.

Competitor Evaluation

Brand Name/ Company Name	Products or Services Offered	Average Price Point	Marketing Attributes	Target Market	Perceived Strengths	Perceived Weaknesses

Unique Selling Point

After you have thoroughly investigated your competitors, it's time to figure out what makes you better/worse/different than they are. Thoroughly understanding what makes your company different will help you develop marketing material that will clearly convey these differences to consumers. It's not an easy task to get a consumer who has been purchasing one type of product or service to switch over and try another company unless you're able to outline what benefits and attributes your products or services offer that competitors' don't.

Using the S.W.O.T. Matrix you created earlier and your Competitor Spreadsheet along with your knowledge of your target market, you can now develop a succinct Unique Selling Point that explains why customers would want to use your company. A Unique Selling Point is the top reason why your target market, based on what you know about them, may switch brands and start purchasing from you. The Unique Selling Point should highlight what makes your products or services different based on the needs and desires that are important to your target audience.

One of the most frequently used examples of a great Unique Selling Point is FedEx's which essentially states "When it absolutely, positively, has to be there overnight." Given that FedEx's target customers are businesses, their Unique Selling Point is a promise to their consumers that important documents will arrive on time. To that target market the guaranteed on-time delivery is paramount – even more important than cost – and it's something that competitors, like the United States Postal Services, can't promise with certainty.

So, as you look at all this information you've completed thus far in the workbook, what is your Unique Selling Point? Your Unique Selling Point should, perhaps after several rewrites, be a concise statement no longer than a sentence as you want it to be something you can easily convey in advertising and in conversations with consumers, and – one day – perhaps even investors.

Unique Selling Point
(Aunt B's Jams)

A new spin on traditional jam flavors, based on the bounty

of locally-sourced Pacific Northwest ingredients

_____

_____

_____

_____

Unique Selling Point
(Drew's Dog Walking Service)

1-hour walks guaranteed to leave active dog breeds bone tired

_____

_____

_____

_____

Positioning Statement - Pulling Together Everything Thus Far

You've done a lot of leg work but now comes the time when you need to take everything you've learned about your target customers; their needs and emotions, as well as what you know about your competitors and be able to communicate your Unique Selling Point to find your niche in the marketplace. The Positioning Statement builds off of your Unique Selling Point; explaining in one cohesive sentence who your target market is and why they'll buy your product or service. Not only will this help you succinctly explain your business concept to friends and family, but also to customers, future employees, vendors you work with, potential partners, etc.

Additionally, every business and marketing decision you make should be looked at through the lens of your Positioning Statement. This will ensure that the new product you're thinking of introducing, the pricing for your services, the marketing materials you're creating, even where to market your products such as which social media tools you should use, is consistent with your Positioning Statement. This simple exercise will help you keep your brand narrowly defined (remember, 'everyone' is not your target audience!), identify what your brand means and how that resonates with customers, and will enable you to create consistent messaging around the brand. Done correctly, that is how people start to associate your brand with certain feelings or emotions and make them want to purchase what you're selling time and time again.

The framework of a classic positioning statement requires identification of the target market, a frame of reference, a primary benefit, and a key attribute. These four parts are combined into one sentence as follows:

Positioning Statement

To (target), (your company) is the brand of (frame of reference) that (primary benefit) because (key attributes).

_____

_____

_____

_____

_____

_____

_____

_____

_____

_____

_____

_____

_____

The **target** is your intended audience or customers; your tightly defined primary target market. Once again, as a small business it's not wise to try to be everything to everyone as that will just create a scattered and confused marketing message. Better to try and become a big fish in a small pond by narrowing down your target audience as tightly as possible.

The **frame of reference** explains what your brand actually is and what niche it competes in. Use the category information you completed earlier in this section.

The **primary benefit** should be the major benefit of your product. Make sure this is a benefit that your target market values because it solves a problem or fills a need. Ideally your primary benefit will also be something that your competitors don't have. As a note, you should avoid putting two primary benefits in your positioning statement because that may clutter your marketing messaging. Oftentimes the primary benefit is actually going to be based on an emotion the customer will feel after buying or using the product and less focused on a tangible benefit. If you, for example, formulated a new form of peppermint spray that was a natural mouse repellent, your primary benefit might be 'let's you feel confident that mice stay outside while kids and pets stay healthy inside.'

Key attributes are the reasons *why* the consumer is going to believe your primary benefit. For example, for that mouse-repelling peppermint spray, the key attributes might be 'made with all-natural ingredients' and 'peppermint repels mice but it's safe for dogs and kids.'

Here's a completed Positioning Statement for that mouse repelling peppermint spray example:

Positioning Statement
Natural Mouse Repellent

To rural families who struggle with mice but don't want to use chemicals for fear it will damage the greater ecosystem (target market – you can see that this is hIghly refined and not just rural families, but rural families that are environmentalists), Mouse-Be-Gone (company) is the brand of mouse and rodent repellant (frame of reference) that let's you feel confident that mice stay outside while kids and pets stay healthy inside (primary benefit) because it's made with all-natural peppermint, an herb that naturally repels mice but is safe for humans and pets (key attribute).

Taking our earlier Aunt B's Jam example, the positioning statement for that company might read something like this:

**Positioning Statement
Aunt B's Jams**

To parents who value organic and handmade ingredients, Aunt B's Jams is the brand of jam and spread that let's them feel good about feeding their children because Aunt B's handcrafts small batches using locally-sourced ingredients from small family-owned farms.

Whereas Drew's Dog Walking Service's positioning statement would be:

Positioning Statement
Drew's Dog Walking Service

To dog-owners of highly athletic avid and large-sized breeds in the Seattle metro area. Drew's Dog Walking Services is a pet care services company that lets dog owners leave their dogs at home guilt free knowing that these dogs will get plenty of exercise and attention.

See, that's not too hard! Creating a Positioning Statement for your small company doesn't have to take a lot of time but it's invaluable when it comes to smart business and marketing decision-making. By comparing your marketing decisions to the Positioning Statement you make sure you're staying 'on brand' in all your messaging and communications with customers. This creates and reinforces consistent associations with your company name, logo, and products in the customers' minds.

Using the following Positioning Statement worksheet and Framework template, craft a positioning statement for your company.

Positioning Statement Worksheet

Who is your target market?_____
What is your frame of reference?_____
What is your product or service's primary benefit?_____

What is your product or service's key attribute?_____
_____

Put these together using the following format as a guideline.
To (target market), (company name or product name) is the brand of (frame of reference) that (primary benefit) because (key attribute).

_____
_____
_____
_____
_____
_____
_____
_____
_____
_____
_____
_____

Positioning Statement

To (target), (your company) is the brand of (frame of reference) that (primary benefit) because (key attributes).

_____
_____
_____
_____
_____
_____
_____
_____
_____
_____
_____

The business school I attended used case studies as its primary teaching method. Business cases look at the circumstances of a real company at some point in time, where it stands in the marketplace at that time, and what problems or challenges the company is trying to overcome at that point in time. Students are required to read through the material and come up with a plan of action – including supporting financial documents on why the company should follow your recommendations.

In my first ever MBA Marketing class we were given a case where a publically-traded company was brining a new product into a highly competitive space. Our assignment was to determine how that new product should be positioned given that it was fairly similar to every other product already on the shelf. How would we convince consumers that they needed to switch brands?

I immediately thought I saw what was the most obvious answer. We should simply undercut our competitors on price. Granted, that means we'd have to take a little less profit on each product sold (since our costs were fairly similar to the costs of our competitors) but so what, we'd surely make it up in volume as customers would switch from other more expensive brands to ours.

And then I got my paper back with less than stellar marks. As we later discussed as a class, the case study company and I had thought the same thing. They'd used low prices alone to differentiate their product from competitors' That all went well for a short time until one of the other competitors got fed up with losing market share and decided to price their product even lower. And so began what's known as 'the race to the bottom' where companies are willing to sacrifice profit margin in order to gain a bigger share of the customer market. In the end, this is usually a losing strategy.

While not the best grade, that paper was a great learning lesson. The reminder of that grade came into play when I was running my own small business – don't let price be your differentiator. You need to price your products in a way that does make sense based on your costs and with price points that your target market will be wiling to pay, but you can't simply let price be the reason why people should buy your product or service over a competitors'. That's a very dangerous game and sooner or later someone will decide to take you up on the challenge and price even lower than you. Then what's your plan?

Customer Emotions, Purchasing Decisions, and Your Marketing Message

Now that you know who your target customers are and what motivations or emotions they're trying to satisfy when purchasing products and services, the next step is to put this information into action in your business. Following are 3 ways this information can benefit your business:

1. The emotions behind why your target customer purchases your products or services should be part of your brand positioning statement. The attributes or benefits you outline in your positioning statement can help your customers 'feel' something that elevates your product or service from a basic commodity to something special.

2. Make these emotions part of your brand identity. Yes, telling your customers about your product attributes is important but so too is connecting with them on an emotional level. You should include aspects of the core customer motivations in your brand identity and your brand messaging. Using the earlier wedding cake example, if you find that most of your customers are buying wedding cakes from you to help them fulfill a desire to feel creative, then you may want to make sure that your logo conveys that artistry and the cake pictures showcased on your website are some of your more creative examples. You may also want to feature stories of wedding couples who you've worked with and focus on those weddings that embody that creativity and artistry.

3. Your brand voice is just as important as your website and pictures. A brand voice is the tone you want to convey when you write your marketing material, when you write the text for your website, and even when you send out a 140-character tweet. If your wedding cake company helps people feel creative then the company's voice also needs to be creative. Perhaps you can achieve this by posting artistic pictures on Instagram or sharing inspirational ideas on Pinterest. Alternatively, a company that helps someone feel sophisticated and professional would have a very different sound to it. Make sure that your brand voice matches your brand identity at all times.

Section Checklist

Understand Who Your Target Market Is

List The Categories Your Company's
Products or Services Fall Under

Create An Ideal Customer Description

Define Your Unique Selling Point

Create Your Positioning Statement

Develop Marketing Strategy and Messaging
Based On That Positioning

SECTION 3: THE FINANCIAL NUTS AND BOLTS

You're starting this business to make money, right? You may not be looking to make millions of dollars and sell to a private equity firm one day (or maybe you are!) but the goal of starting a business is to take your ideas, energy, passion, and ideas and turn them into a personally rewarding and profitable endeavor. Oftentimes though, the financial piece of the business plan is the one that people are least excited about but it's certainly important. How can you expect to make money if you don't understand the financials of the business model you're pulling together?

> The IRS looks for profitability too if you're hoping to deduct business expenses from your personal income tax return. The IRS says that the difference between a business and a hobby is that a business will be profitable in three out of five years. If your business doesn't end up meeting these qualifications the IRS may decide that you are a hobbyist and that will change the deductions you can legally claim on your tax return.

Putting A Positive Spin on the Financials

If you're not jumping up and down with excitement about tackling the financial part of your business plan, let's look at this in a different way. Working through the financials now enables you to see whether the business model you're planning to implement is going to payoff in the way you hope. If it turns out, through this process, you discover that the plans you have aren't going to pan out financially based on your earlier stated business goals, you now have the opportunity to go back and make changes to your assumptions *before* you start putting any time, energy, and money into implementing your plan. Isn't that better than getting part way through the year and then realizing that everything you've done over the last few months isn't actually going to move the needle for your business as you thought it would?

Financial Tools

If you're familiar with Excel, you may choose to work through the following exercises using that tool by recreating the templates within an Excel spreadsheet which you can then use to input your financial assumptions and play with the data. Many times part of the hesitation entrepreneurs have about working on the financials is an apprehension about being forced to use Excel. If this is you, don't worry! While it will undoubtedly be useful to your business if you become more comfortable with Excel at some point (you might be able to find low-priced, one-day classes at your local community college continuing education department, online tutorials, or classes through your library), you don't necessarily need to know how to use Excel to get through this part of the workbook. Simply use the templates provided and a calculator in this section to help guide your thinking and create a financial model you can work with.

While not needed for completing your business plan, having an accounting and bookkeeping program in place from Day 1 is integral to businesses everywhere. QuickBooks is one of the best small business accounting software tools available though other options such as Wave and Xero are also popular amongst entrepreneurs. As you start to incur business expenses and generate revenue, you will need a way to keep all of the financials of your business organized. These bookkeeping programs and other like them will not only help you keep things organized, but if kept up to date, it can also run reports that tell you how your business is performing (which you can use to measure against your goals) and can provide you with the information you need to file taxes with. If you are not familiar with business bookkeeping, it is a worthwhile investment to take a class (again, classes can be found at your local community college, online, or through libraries) so that you understand the basics of the software program.

Speaking of bookkeeping, if accounting is one aspect of entrepreneurship that is not your strong suit, a good bookkeeper or accountant is worth their weight in gold when it comes to keeping the finances of your business organized, up-to-date, and helping you make sure all the appropriate business taxes, including payroll and sales taxes as applicable, are paid on time. An experienced bookkeeper or accountant who has worked with small businesses is one of the best investments you can make for the future of your business. The financials of your business are simply too important to ignore as they are the main predictor of the health of your business.

Ok, let's dive into the financial section!

How Much Does Your Product or Service Cost You? Determining Your Cost Of Goods Sold (COGS)

Depending on what it is your business is selling — be it handknit baby sweaters, handmade jewelry, or graphic design services — you need to understand how much your products or services cost you before you can determine what price to charge for them. Many times entrepreneurs fall into the trap of approaching this backwards; determining what their price will be based on what they think someone will pay or based on what their competitors are charging. This is a dangerous way to price your products or services because you're arriving at a number without a solid understanding of how much it costs you to produce that product or provide that service. You will always struggle with profitability if this is how you approach pricing because you may, unknowingly, be pricing your products in a way that provides you with little to no profit when all your direct costs and indirect expenses are taken into account.

In order to determine what your costs are, you need to account for the costs that are directly related to your product or service. At this point we're not yet including things like your marketing costs or your overhead such as monthly office rent or phone bill, but only those variable costs that can be directly tied to the production of products or services. For example, in our dog walker example we've listed things like the gas needed for the van to and from the dogs' homes and the park as well as dog treats and report cards for each of the dogs. For the product provider, in this case our jam maker, the variable costs are things like her ingredients and packaging. Take a minute to think through what variable costs, in your case, go into the making of your product or providing of your service and list them in the Directly Related Product/Services Costs worksheet. You may want to make copies of the blank worksheet if you have multiple products or services and use one worksheet per product or service.

Fixed vs. Variable Costs

You will hear the terms 'fixed' and 'variable' used a lot in business accounting so it's worthwhile to spend a minute understanding the difference between them. Fixed Costs are those costs that your business incurs regardless of whether or not you have any sales. For example, things like your telephone bill, your business licenses, you car insurance (in the case of the dog walker), your commercial kitchen rent (in the case of the jam maker), etc. are all fixed costs. Those bills come due on a regular basis regardless of whether you've worked with 1000 clients or sold 1000 units that month or sold nothing at all.

Variable Costs are those expenses that are directly tied to your produce or service sales. As your sales increase so too do your variable costs and when your sales slow down you variable costs decrease as well. For example, for our dog walker, things like gas and dog treats would be variable costs. The more dog-walking clients Drew has, the more he has to spend on gas and dog treats. For product providers like our jam company, variable costs are those thing you physically have to have on hand in order to make the products – such as yarn if you're a knitter, wood if you're a furniture carpenter, or ingredients for food product providers. As you make more products because your sales are increasing then you will need more yarn, more wood, more ingredients, etc., and your variable costs will increase. But as you make and sell less products then you need less of those items and your variable costs will decrease.

Labor, be it your hours or those of an employee, is also technically a variable cost because the more products you need or more clients you work with, the more hours you and any employee will have to work so your labor costs will increase. But if no one's buying your products or no one needs your services then your labor costs will decrease because business is slow.

Directly Related Product/Services Costs

Directly Related Product/Services Costs
(Aunt B's Jams)

produce

mason jars

sugar

decorative ribbon

gelatin

Directly Related Product/Services Costs
(Drew's Dog Walking Service)

gas for dog pickups

daily report cards

dog treats

Calculating Your Product Costs

For product businesses like Aunt B's Jams that produces and sells physical products, knowing how much it costs to make these items is the most critical component of your business plan. In order to create the product that they sell, these business owners have to pay money up front for raw materials. So for a jeweler, this means paying in advance for the gold that she'll turn into bracelets and sell, the fashion designer must pay upfront for fabric before he can bring his designs to life, and the soap maker needs lye, oils, and essences in order to produce beautiful-smelling bars of soap, etc. If any of these product producers don't understand all the costs that go into their finished products then how can they price their products in a way that they're confident of making money?

When determining your product costs, you should only take into account those costs that are directly tied to the products you create so in the case of the jeweler, this would mean that the jeweler would account for the costs of the gold wire she uses and the beads but not the machinery and tools she uses to craft her jewelry. She would also take into account the packaging she puts the jewelry in because it's a variable cost that is directly tied to the sale of that product. Let's take a look at this example in more detail.

Joanna is a jeweler and wants to know how much her dangly gold earrings cost her to make. She knows that each earring uses 2 inches of gold wire which she buys for $13/foot and 1 glass bead which she can buy for $20 (per 100 beads). Each pair of earrings also has two earring backs which cost her $.1 per set of backings and she packages them in a tin gift box with a clear top which costs her $40 for 1000 boxes and ties the box with 4 inches of purple ribbon which costs her $4.90 for 25 yards. How much do the earrings cost her to make?

Product Costing
(Joanna's Jewelry)

Basic Raw Materials Cost

Gold Wire = $13/foot = $13/12inches = $1.08 per inch

Glass Beads = $20/100 beads = $2 per bead

Earrings Backs = $.1/set of backings

Tin Gift Set = $40/100 boxes = $4 per box

Purple Ribbon = $4.90/25 yards = $4.90/900 inches
= $.005 per inch

Product Raw Materials Cost

2 inches x 2 earrings = 2 x (2 x $1.08) = $4.32

1 bead x 2 earrings = $.40

1 set of backings = $.1

1 box = $.4

4 inches of ribbon = 4 x $.005 = $.02

Add Product Raw Materials Costs Together = $5.24

Based on the example above, it costs Joanna $5.24 in product costs to produce one set of these earrings. But what about her time? We haven't taken that into account yet. Assuming that it takes Joanna 3 hours to create these earrings and she values her time at $20/hour then her labor costs would be $60. This would adjust her product cost significantly:

Associated Raw Materials Cost = $5.24

Total Labor Cost = $60.00

Total Product Cost = $65.24

So in this case, Joanna needs to charge a minimum of $65.24 just to break even on her variable product costs. If she charges less than that then she's effectively saying that her time is worth less. Alternatively, it's not uncommon for entrepreneurs to charge so little for their product that not only are their labor costs not accounted for, but neither are all of the product costs. The last thing you want to be doing as a small business owner is actually spending more to make your products than you're charging for them because that's not a business model that will last very long! Since you, like Joanna our jeweler, probably have more than one product that you're selling or that you plan to sell, make sure you walk through this exercise for each product you offer.

Product Costing

Product Name:

_____

Basic Raw Materials Cost

_____
_____
_____
_____
_____
_____
_____
_____
_____
_____

Product Raw Materials Cost

_____
_____
_____
_____
_____
_____
_____
_____
_____
_____

Total Associated Raw Materials Cost _____

Total Labor Cost _____

Total Product Cost _____

**Per piece cost if more than one unit
is produced at a time** _____

Product Costing
(Aunt B's Jams)

Product Name:

Strawberry Vanilla Jam

Raw Materials Cost

2 Quarts Strawberries = $5.29 per quart

1 kg Sugar = $.67 per kg

2 Vanilla Beans = $38/100 beans = $.38 per bean

2 Lemons = $1.09 per lemon

6 oz Liquid Pectin = $2.99/12 oz = $.25 per oz

4 Pint Jars = $5.99/12 jars = $.49 per jar

4 Labels = $11.75/100 labels = $.11 per label

Associated Raw Materials Cost

2 quarts × $3.29 = $6.58

1 × $.67 = $.67

2 vanilla beans × $.38 = $.76

2 lemons × $1.09 = $2.18

6 ounces × $.25 = $1.50

4 jars × $.83 = $1.96

4 labels × $.11 = $.44

Total Associated Raw Materials Cost = $14.09

Total Labor Cost = $24.00
(It takes Aunt B's 2 hours to make this jam at $12.00/hr)

Total Product Cost = $38.09

In this case, this Total Product Cost refers to the total cost to make 4 jars so the cost per jar cost is $9.52.

Services provider types vary widely and as such their costs can vary too. Someone like a freelance social media consultant or contract bookkeeper may have minimal directly related costs since things like office rent and advertising expenses don't correlate directly to their cost of providing the service. For a service provider of this type, the time it takes him or her to work with clients is a directly related cost. In this case, the costing exercise is fairly simple as you just need to determine what you value one hour of your time at pricewise. One way to look at this is to determine how much you'd like the business to make, revenue-wise by the end of the year. Remember that this is what the business will make before other costs are taken into account so if a consultant actually wants to make $X at the end of the year, net of the expenses, then s/he will have to increase business goal by $X + business expenses (we will work through business expenses in the next section so you can always come back and revise this worksheet as needed).

First, determine how many hours in the year that you would be working. This is a great time to refer back to your Vision Statement. If you'd ideally like to be able to take a few weeks off in the Summer to spend time fly-fishing then make sure you're not calculating those weeks into this equation. As a note, assuming a 40-hour work week with 2 weeks off every year brings you to 2000 hours annually so add or subtract from there as needed. However, you can't assume that all of those hours will be spent working with clients or working on projects. You have to devote some of your time to basic administrative tasks like bookkeeping, invoicing clients, answering emails, and doing your own marketing to help bring in future business. The traditional model assumes that you will spend about 30% of your time on these tasks so you should take your total annual hours and multiply them by the actual time you will be working with clients' projects. Then divide the total business revenue goal by the actual billable hours to reach determine your cost per hour.

Services Costing
(Social Media Mike)

Mike is a social media consultant who helps small businesses build and maintain their social media presence. He wants his business to earn $100,000 annually. He also wants to be able to take 4 weeks off every year and work a half day on Fridays in order to spend more time with his family. How much does he need to charge per hour in order to reach that goal?

Work Hours: 48 weeks worked out of 52 total x 35 hours per week = 1,680 hours

Billable Hours: 1,680 hours with 30% dedicated to administrative tasks =

$$(1,680 \times .3) = 504 \text{ administrative hours}$$
$$1,680-504 = 1,176 \text{ billable hours}$$

Necessary Hourly Rate: $100,000/1,176 = $85.04

Other types of service providers will have costs associated with some of the services they offer. A hair dresser for example has to pay for the shampoo, conditioner, hair dye, and foils as well as the mousse that goes into their clients' hair during styling. A daycare may need to feed the children during the day which is a cost they incur and even our dog walker has costs associated to each dog he walks, as illustrated by the Directly Related Product/Services Costs worksheet because of the gas needed to drive, the dog treats he hands out, and the daily report cards he leaves at each client's home.

For these service providers, the cost of their products is the combination of their hourly rate plus those costs that are directly attributable to the service they're providing. For example, Drew the dog walker would calculate his hourly rate the same way as the social media consultant too but since he can take multiple dogs out at once, he would divide his rate by the number of dogs she has and then add in his directly related costs.

Services Costing
(Drew's Dog Walking Service)

Drew wants to make $50,000 annually and plans on working 5 days a week with two weeks off every year. He makes multiple park trips each day with each trip taking 2.5 hours and he takes a total of 6 dogs on each trip. Each dog receives a treat and a report card indicating how the dog behaved that day. Drew has also calculated that he spends $1.25 per dog on gas.

Work Hours: 50 weeks worked out of 52 × 40 hours per week = 2,000 hours

Billable Hours: 2,000 hours with 20% dedicated to administrative tasks

(2,000 × .2) = 400 administrative hours

2,000 - 400 = 1,600 billable hours

Hourly Rate: $50,000 / 1,600 = $31.25

Time per service (each park trip in this case): $31.25 × 2.5 = $78.12

Cost per dog for one park trip: $78.12/6 dogs = $13.02

Additional Associated Costs (per dog): $.32 dog treat

$.16 report card

$1.25 gas

Total Additional Associated Costs (per dog): $1.73

Total Cost Per Dog: $13.02 + $1.73 = $14.75

Now it's your turn. Use the following blank worksheet to determine what your services cost you. If your services don't have any directly related costs (you're more like our social media consultant) then just complete the worksheet up through the Hourly Rate calculation. All others who do have directly related costs should complete the entire worksheet. In the latter case, if you offer multiple services and each has different directly related costs make sure to complete one worksheet per service.

Services Costing

Service Name:

_____

Work Hours: _____ = _____

Billable Hours: _____

_____

_____

Hourly Rate: _____ = _____

Additional Directly Related Costs

_____ = _____

_____ = _____

_____ = _____

_____ = _____

_____ = _____

_____ = _____

Total Additional Costs = _____

Hours Required to Complete Service x Hourly Rate _____ x _____ = _____

Total Additional Costs + _____

Total Additional Costs + _____

Pricing Your Products/Services Appropriately

You've just calculated your costs for your products or services (which is also known as your Cost of Goods Sold), but how do we determine what you're going to price those products and services to your customers? And what about those overhead, marketing, and other costs that weren't taken into account in our earlier calculations? This section is where we'll tackle those important questions.

Most first-time entrepreneurs, eager to make their first sale and get their business underway, rush through pricing to arrive at a final price that's typically some combination of guessing what they think customers would actually pay and a rough idea of what it actually costs them to produce the goods or deliver the service. That's a dangerous tactic to take because once you set your prices it's hard to raise them without explaining to your customers why you're doing so. And if your customers have gotten used to buying your product or service at $Y price, how do you think they'll react to price increases? Will they start looking elsewhere? Product pricing deserves some careful thinking on your part.

Other Pricing Considerations

- Some entrepreneurs base their prices off what their competitors are charging. While you need to be very aware of what your competitors' prices are and, as such, how much you think customers in your area are willing to pay for a product or service like yours, you can't simply assume that your competitor has done their homework. What's more, you and your competitor might have very different cost structures – maybe Aunt B's uses organic strawberries which are more expensive than the traditionally grown strawberries her competitors are using. Perhaps Drew's Dog Walking Service's main competitor drives an electronic car so doesn't have a gas expense like Drew. Simply going off of the pricing of your competitors without knowing your own Cost of Goods Sold can set you up for failure.

- If you choose your price without understanding all of your costs then you may not be building in enough of a cushion to account for all those pieces of running your business that aren't associated with your Costs of Goods Sold (like all those other costs of running your business).
- If your business is the type that could grow into other markets or other distribution channels down the road (for example, you may start off selling your product at farmers' markets or craft fairs but dream of selling it into local retail boutiques as well one day), the price you charge needs to give you enough margin or profit so that when you start working with retailers, for instance, you're able to provide them with a wholesale price. Essentially, the wholesale price is a discounted price to the retailer who makes money by buying your product at the wholesale price and then selling it to the customer at the retail price. The difference between the two is where the retailer makes a profit. You, however, need to make sure that the wholesale price is still providing you with a comfortable profit margin for every item you sell. Similarly, a service provider who's currently working out of a home office but one day wants to rent a downtown office (that's what he had in his Vision Statement!) needs to make sure that he's charging appropriately now so that he can afford that downtown rent in the future.

Pricing for Products Companies

Suggested Retail Price

This is where your Vision Statement really comes in handy. If your Vision Statement had you making your products and selling them directly to consumers (via farmer's markets/festivals/events, your own storefront, and/or online through your own e-commerce store) and you have no plans to sell wholesale to stores, catalogues companies, or other online retailers, then to determine your retail price you simply take the Cost of Goods Sold that you've calculated for each product and add a healthy margin to it. The margin percentage, which you determine, gets built into the product price in order to help cover those fixed expenses your business incurs (like that rent we keep talking about or that phone bill, etc.) and those variable costs (like Marketing expenses such as advertising) that aren't directly related to the product to make sure that your company is profitable.

What's a good margin? Most experts would say that a good back-of-the-envelope calculation is to start by assuming a 60-70% margin unless your fixed and other variable costs are significantly higher than other similar businesses. Let's see how this would look under this scenario:

Product Price Calculator
(Retail Only)

Total Product Cost (COGS) per unit $2.50

Desired Margin 60%

COGS/(1-margin) $2.50/(1-.60) = $6.25

Retail Price $6.25

Profit (Retail Price - COGS) $6.25 - $2.50 = $3.75

As you can see, based on desired margins of 60% and COGS of $2.50, this product company should charge $6.25 for each unit of product sold and that would provide them with a profit of $3.75. That profit is what will help pay for their other non-related costs and what's left over can go into the company owner's pocket or put back into the business to invest in future growth.

Keep in mind that this $6.25 is just a starting point though. Go back to your Competitive Analysis spreadsheet and see how your pricing equates to those of your competitors. Is the pricing that your considering significantly higher or lower than your competitors? If its significantly higher than you need to ask yourself whether customers will pay the difference between your price and a competitors (hint – in order to get them to do so you must clearly convey to them what makes your product so much better). Alternatively, you might need to see if there are ways to lower your product cost by using different raw materials or determine whether you're willing to accept a smaller margin on your products. If your price is lower than your competitors', you might want to consider raising your prices and thus giving yourself more margin. Prices that are significantly lower than competitors can be perceived by customers as having subpar quality and that is not something you would necessarily want associated with your brand.

Wholesale and Retail Pricing

If you outlined in your Vision Statement is that you plan to sell your products wholesale to stores, either exclusively or in combination with selling directly to customers yourself, then there's another layer of pricing that needs to be considered. Understandably, stores don't want to buy your product at your retail price and then mark it up from there so that they can make a profit. So, in effect, you will have a two-tier pricing structure; your wholesale price, which you offer to stores, and your suggested retail price which is the price you sell your products to customers at farmers' markets, online, etc. at and is also the price you recommend that stores use as well. Note, however, the word 'suggested' – this means that it is the price you can recommend but you can't require that stores abide by that pricing and they can price as they see fit once the product is in their control.

To create these two tiers of pricing it's best to start by working with the wholesale price first since the suggested retail price is built off of that. Starting with our Total Product Cost worksheet, we add a margin percentage which will reasonably cover your other costs and still give you a satisfactory profit. In an ideal world, you should shoot to have wholesale margins of 50%, but that does vary depending on what your products you're producing and you may find that your margins are significantly higher or lower and is still in-line with prices that customers are willing to pay. At its most basic, you want to make sure that your wholesale margin will help cover your overhead costs and provide you with a profit. Let's look at Aunt B's example:

Wholesale to Retail
Product Price Calculator
(Aunt B's Jams)

Product Name:

Strawberry Vanilla Jam

Total Product Cost (COGS) per unit $9.52

Desired Wholesale Margin 30%

COGS/(1-margin) $9.52/(1-.3) = $13.60

Wholesale Price $13.60

Profit (Wholesale Price-COGS) $4.08

Wholesale Price $13.60

Desired Retail Margin 50%

Wholesale Price/(1-desired margin) $13.60/(1-.5) = $27.20

Suggested Retail Price $27.20

Later in this section we'll discuss what to do if you find your ideal pricing is too high for customers.

Under this scenario, Aunt B's has determined that she can take a smaller margin percentage. Be careful though before you give all your margin away as you'll be surprised by how quickly that money disappears once all your other business expenses are accounted for.

Once the wholesale price has been determined, Aunt B is able to figure out what her suggested retail price should be. Keep in mind that even if stores ask you for the suggested retail price (SRP), they may price it above or below that depending on their specific pricing strategy and customer base. It's safe to assume, however, that most retailers want a 50% margin themselves above the wholesale price so when in doubt use that percentage. This is important because they not only want to know that the product will sell but that they're using their shelf space efficiently and getting the maximum margin they can comparable to other products in their store.

Retail or Wholesale to Retail? Not sure which pricing method to use?

If you plan on one day selling to retail stores, it's best to use the Wholesale to Retail Product Price Calculation method as it will provide you with the room to grow your business into retail channels when you're ready. In the meantime, it provides you with more profit to keep for yourself and use to grow your business.

Wholesale to Retail Product Price Calculations

Product Name:

_____

Total Product Cost (COGS) per unit _____

Desired Wholesale Margin _____

COGS/(1-margin) _____ / (1-   ) = _____

Wholesale Price _____

Profit (Wholesale Price-COGS) _____

Wholesale Price _____

Desired Retail Margin _____

Wholesale Price/(1-desired margin) _____ / (1-   ) = _____

Suggested Retail Price _____

Pricing for Services Companies

Determining the pricing for services companies is somewhat easier than products companies. Earlier, in the Services Costing worksheet, we figured out how much you'd need to earn in order to provide yourself with a specific salary by determining what hourly rate you need to charge based on the number of actual billable hours per year you anticipate working.

To determine your pricing, you need to add to that salary figure the estimated annual cost of your other business expenses – things like your rent, office supplies, and marketing expenses and then walk back through your Product Costing exercise again. Using this methodology, you can determine what your hourly rate should be in order to help you reach your salary goal and take into account all of your business expenses. For example, earlier we looked at our freelance social media consultant Bob who wanted to earn $100,000. (As a note, you may want to wait and return to this section after completing the Monthly Expense Worksheet later in this section.)

Services Costing
(Social Media Mike)

Mike is a social media consultant who helps small businesses build and maintain their social media presence. He wants his business to earn $100,000 annually. He also wants to be able to take 4 weeks off every year and work a half day on Fridays in order to spend more time with his family. How much does he need to charge per hour in order to reach that goal?

Work Hours: 48 weeks worked out of 52 total x 35 hours per week = 1,680 hours

Billable Hours: 1,680 hours with 30% dedicated to administrative tasks =

$$(1,680 \times .3) = 504 \text{ administrative hours}$$

$$1,680 - 504 = 1,176 \text{ billable hours}$$

Necessary Hourly Rate: $100,000 / 1,176 = $85.04

But Bob also calculates that he's going to have about $15,000 in business expenses each year and he doesn't want that to cut into his take-home salary. Therefore, he needs to go back and work through the costing exercise again, this time taking into account that additional $15,000 in anticipated expenses.

Services Pricing Example

Work Hours: 48 weeks worked out of 52 total x 35 hours per week = 1680 hours

Billable Hours : 1680 hours with 30% dedicated to administrative tasks
(1680 x .3) = 504 administrative hours
1680-504=1176 billable hours

Necessary Hourly Rate ($100,000 + 15,000)/1176 = $97.78

In the case of a service provider like Drew who has some directly related business expenses in addition to overhead and other fixed business expenses that he's anticipating, the business expenses are computed in with his desired salary from which his hourly rate is derived and from there the other directly related costs are added on top.

Services Costing
(Drew's Dog Walking Service)

Drew wants to make $50,000 annually and plans on working 5 days a week with two weeks off every year. He makes multiple park trips each day with each trip taking 2.5 hours and he takes a total of 6 dogs on each trip. Each dog receives a treat and a report card indicating how the dog behaved that day. Drew has also calculated that he spends $1.25 per dog on gas.

Work Hours: 50 weeks worked out of 52 × 40 hours per week = 2,000 hours

Billable Hours: 2,000 hours with 20% dedicated to administrative tasks

$(2000 \times .2) = 400$ administrative hours

$2000 - 400 = 1600$ billable hours

Hourly Rate: $50,000 salary + 10,000 business expenses/1,600 = $37.50

Time per service (each park trip in this case): $37.50 × 2.5 = $93.75

Cost per dog for one park trip: $93.75/6 dogs = $15.62

Additional Associated Costs (per dog): $.32 dog treat

$.16 report card

$.48

Total Cost Per Dog: $15.62 + $.48 = $16.10

Services Costing

Service Name:

_____

Work Hours: _____ = _____

Billable Hours: _____

_____

_____

Hourly Rate: _____ = _____

Additional Directly Related Costs

_____ = _____

_____ = _____

_____ = _____

_____ = _____

_____ = _____

_____ = _____

Total Additional Costs = _____

Hours Required to Complete Service x Hourly Rate _____ x _____ = _____

Total Additional Costs + _____

Total Additional Costs + _____

Understanding Start-up Costs

If you already have your business up and running, this section may not be as pertinent to you as other sections, but for anyone working their way through this workbook who hasn't gotten too far down the entrepreneurial road yet, it's important to understand and anticipate what your start-up costs will be. No matter how small of a business you're planning to start, there's simply no way around the fact that you're going to incur some start-up costs before you can start to produce and sell your products or services. Knowing about these costs in advance allows you to budget for them and not be caught off guard. Nobody likes to be surprised by an expense they didn't anticipate and the purpose of this section is to help you to make sure that doesn't happen. Taking the time to think through all aspects of your business so you can anticipate and plan for your startup expenses in order to manage your cash flow and ensure you have enough funds in the bank to operate and grow.

Because every business is different, you might spend more or less than another business getting started and there's no actual right answer here. You should however take the time to try and make accurate estimates what each of the following categories will cost you. Using the following worksheet, input your estimated costs next to each of the expense items that are outlined. Space is left at the bottom for any expenses that aren't highlighted that your specific business will have to incur. Leave those expenses that don't pertain to your business blank or write N/A for Not Applicable.

Estimated Start-Up Expenses

Business Licenses	$
Additional Permits as Required	$
Basic Marketing Pieces (Logo Design, Branding, etc.)	$
Equipment	$
Website Design	$
Insurance	$
Down Payment on Office or Workspace	$
Telepone/Computer/Internet	$
Office Supplies	$
Professional Fees (Legal, Accounting/etc.)	$
	$
	$
	$
	$
	$
	$
Total	$

Some of these are regularly reoccurring expenses such as monthly office rent, your annual business insurance cost, and your business licenses which you have to resubmit every year. These should be accounted in your Start-up expenses calculations because these are costs you have to pay for before starting your business. However, since they are also on-going, be it either weekly, monthly, or yearly expenses, you will want to make sure they're added into your long-range cash forecast as well that we'll work through soon.

Be realistic when you're making estimates on your startup costs, basing them as much as possible on the expected real costs. If you're not sure, do your homework by asking around to try and get a sense of what that costs. For example, if you're planning to develop your website yourself then your website costs might just include your domain name and any hosting costs. If you're planning to hire someone to build your site, even if it's a friend who's willing to charge you a minimal amount, then you need to take those costs into account. When in doubt, make some calls and get estimates so that you have an idea of what you can realistically expect to pay.

The reason you want to estimate your start-up costs as closely as possible is that you don't want to be surprised with a large cost that you didn't anticipate. At the start of every business money is pretty tight and being a few hundred or even thousand dollars off your estimate could mean the difference between renting that office space you want and working out of your garage.

If, as you look at your completed Start-up worksheet, the number you see at the bottom of the page makes you cringe, now is the time to go back and figure out how you're going to get the money to finance this new business or where you might need to reduce your expenses in order to make this work. There are some expenses, like your business licensing fees, that are an unavoidable cost of doing business, but there may be other areas where you can save money such as keeping the computer you have, even if it is painfully slow, rather than upgrading to a new model. You can always upgrade later once your business has gotten safely onto its feet.

Estimated Monthly Expenses

Using your startup spreadsheet as the foundation, we're now going to determine what you anticipate your monthly operating expenses will be. Operating expenses are those costs that your business incurs on a regular basis to simply keep the business running; things like any monthly rent, your website maintenance costs, your labor costs, etc. These expenses can either be fixed, like the monthly rent or they can be variable, like your labor costs which may increase when you're busier with more sales and decrease during slower periods.

The Start-up Estimate you developed in the last section is the perfect place to start when developing your Estimated Monthly Operating Expenses. Look through your completed Start-up Expense worksheet and determine which of the expenses you outlined are true one-time only costs and which are ongoing expenses your business will encounter on a regular basis. Once again, the rent we mentioned is an ongoing expense so you would want to add it to your Estimated Monthly Operating Costs but a security deposit you needed to pay on the space is a true one-time Start-up Cost since you won't need to pay a security deposit again. Therefore, you can leave the security deposit and other one-time expenses off of your Estimated Monthly Operating Costs worksheet. Similarly, perhaps you purchased a business cell phone, separate from your home number, so that a client calling wouldn't be greeted by your children picking up the phone. When you purchased the new phone you likely had to pay for the equipment which is a one-time startup cost. But going forward you're going to have to pay your monthly telephone bill so that's an ongoing operating expense you need to account for.

Using the following worksheet as a guide, fill in the operating expenses you think your business will encounter on a monthly basis. There are extra blank lines so that you can add in categories that aren't already included that are specific to your business. Similarly, any categories on the worksheet that don't pertain to you simply leave blank.

It can be hard to estimate how much you will spend each month when all of this is new to you and it can be tempting to pull your 'best guess' numbers out of the air and plug them in. I'd caution you against this. When we do that, we have a tendency to 'guesstimate' numbers that are in our favor. In the case of operating expenses, we choose numbers that end up being far below what we'll really end up paying. The idea with this exercise is to try and get your worksheet to accurately list and forecast your monthly expenses so that you plan in advance how you're going to manage these costs. It will also help show you what level of sales volume you need in order to start earning a profit. When in doubt, spend some time doing some research to try and get numbers that are as reasonably accurate as possible. For example, if you know that you want to rent office space but haven't yet found the right spot, ask a realtor what average rents are in your area for the square footage you're looking for. As far as the business cell phone example, you can easily go online to get a better sense of what various cell phone plans will cost you every month.

There are, undoubtedly, some expenses that you simply can't find an accurate number for until you get into the day-to-day running of your business. How much will you be spending on office expenses? It seems like a simple question but most of us have probably never really paid attention to how much we spend when we stop by an office supply store since it's not a regular shopping destination like the grocery store. In cases like this you do have to go with your best estimate based on what you anticipate buying and how much those items, on average, cost.

If you're working through this workbook and already have an existing business in place you are at an advantage because you can review your previous records to find out how much all of these expenses are costing you. It's always better to use real numbers based on your actual experience wherever possible.

As you think about what your expenses would be every month, remember that there are some expenses that are exclusively start-up expenses and you won't have to pay for them again after that first month and others that are ongoing. Lastly, don't forget that your variable expenses are those that rise as your sales rise (and vice versa). If you anticipate strong holiday sales then your variable costs in that month would also increase. On the flip side, if you're Drew the dog walker and everyone goes out of town for the Summer then your sales would decrease but so too would variable costs. Make sure you account for that when filling out your Monthly Estimated Expenses worksheet.

Please note that only the first few months are shown here due to space constraints. Assuming that your business is a year-round business, you should make a copy of this spreadsheet and create at least 12 months' worth of estimated expenses as there may be some differences month to month. If, however, your business is seasonal, you only need to input estimated expenses for those months that your business would be open and operational. Make additional copies as needed to complete your expense spreadsheet.

Monthly Estimated Expenses

Month:

Fixed Costs							
Office/Facilities Rent							
Telephone/Internet							
Accounting Fees							
Total Fixed Costs							
(Add all fixed costs together)							
Variable Costs							
Raw Materials/Direct Product Costs							
Marketing							
Association Fees							
Print Marketing							
Online Marketing							
Website							
Payroll							
Office Supplies							
Total Variable Costs							
(Add all variable costs together)							
Other Costs							
Business Licenses							
Other Permits							
Legal fees							
Total Other Costs							
(Add all other costs together)							
Total Monthly Estimated Expenses							
(Add Total Fixed, Total Variable, and Total Other together)							

Monthly Estimated Expenses
(Aunt B's Jams)

Month:	Startup	April	May	June	July	Aug	Sept
Fixed Costs							
Office/Facilities Rent	$250	$250	$250	$250	$250	$250	$250
Telephone/Internet	$115	$115	$115	$115	$115	$115	$115
Accounting Fees	$30	$30	$30	$30	$30	$30	$30
Total Fixed Costs	$395	$395	$395	$395	$395	$395	$395
(Add all fixed costs together)							
Variable Costs							
Raw Materials/Direct Product Costs	$125	$125	$150	$250	$250	$300	$300
Marketing							
Association Fees	$30	$30	$30	$30	$30	$30	$30
Print Marketing	-	-	-	-	-	-	-
Online Marketing	$25	$25	$25	$25	$25	$25	$25
Website	-	-	-	-	-	-	-
Payroll	$1,500	-	-	-	-	-	-
Office Supplies	$25	$25	$25	$25	$25	$25	$25
Total Variable Costs	$1,705	$205	$230	$330	$330	$380	$380
(Add all variable costs together)							
Other Costs							
Business Licenses	$150	-	-	-	-	-	-
Other Permits	$400	-	-	-	-	-	-
Legal fees	-	-	-	-	-	-	-
Total Other Costs	$550	0	0	0	0	0	0
(Add all other costs together)							
Total Monthly Estimated Expenses	$2,650	$600	$625	$725	$725	$775	$775
(Add Total Fixed, Total Variable, and Total Other together)							

Monthly Estimated Expenses
(Drew's Dog Walking Service)

Month:	Startup	Jan	Feb	March	April	May	June
Fixed Costs							
Office/Facilities Rent	-	-	-	-	-	-	-
Telephone/Internet	$150	$150	$150	$150	$150	$150	$150
Accounting Fees	$30	$30	$30	$30	$30	$30	$30
Total Fixed Costs	$180	$180	$180	$180	$180	$180	$180
(Add all fixed costs together)							
Variable Costs							
Raw Materials/Direct Product Costs	-	$12	$12	$40	$40	$50	$50
Marketing							
Association Fees	$30	$30	$30	$30	$30	$30	$30
Print Marketing	-	$150		$150		$150	
Online Marketing	-	$40	$40	$40	$40	$40	$40
Website	$3,000	-	-	-	-	-	-
Payroll	-	-	-	-	-	-	-
Office Supplies	$25	$25	$25	$25	$25	$25	$25
Gas	$0	$15	$22	$74	$168	$212	$428
Total Variable Costs	$3,055	$272	$129	$359	$303	$507	$573
(Add all variable costs together)							
Other Costs							
Business Licenses	$150						
Other Permits	$400						
Legal fees	$300						
Insurance	$45	$45	$45	$45	$45	$45	$45
Total Other Costs	$895	$45	$45	$45	$45	$45	$45
(Add all other costs together)							
Total Monthly Estimated Expenses	$4,130	$497	$354	$584	$528	$732	$798
(Add Total Fixed, Total Variable, and Total Other together)							

Determining Your Break-Even: Making Sure Any Of This Is Realistic!

Now, based on your assumptions, the Monthly Estimated Expense Worksheet tells you how much you'll expect to spend on operating expenses every month. The next question then is, based on those total expenses (both fixed and variable), how much do you need to earn on sales to break-even.

Break-even refers to the point where the total expenses of your business equals the revenue your business generates and you are neither losing nor making money. Granted, the point is to actually make money but before you can get there you need to know where that tipping point is between your costs and your revenue.

Break-even for Services Companies

Let's start first by taking a look at a services company that charges by the billable hour, like a graphic designer or consultant. This is the simplest of scenarios to figure out; simply divide your average Monthly

Estimated Expenses by your preferred hourly rate (based on the information you calculated earlier). The result is the number of hours you need to work every month in order to break-even.

If you're a services company, like Drew's Dog Walking Service, that provides services at a set rate rather than an hourly fee, then you need to take you Monthly Estimated Expenses and divide them by the average cost for your services. Drew, for example, offers 30 minute dog walking at $25 per half-hour, 60-minute dog walking at $35 per hour. To get his average hourly rate for services, Drew uses the following calculations:

$25/half hour x 2 = $50/hour for 30 min walks

$35/hour for 60 min walks

$85/hour

To get this average fee, he divides $85 by the number of services he offers (in this case, two).

$85/2 = $42.50

Why We Use Average Rate/Price

When you're trying to determine your break-even point and you have multiple price points because of different products or services you offer, you should take the average of those prices to give you a ballpark price for each unit sold or hour billed. If, however, you've already been operating and have historical data that can provide guidance about what products or services are the most popular then you should use that information o calculate what percentage of your sales come from each price point and then take the weighted average of those numbers.

Average Price Point With No Historical Data

Price Points: $3.50, $6.00, $4.95

($3.50+$6.00+$4.75)/3 - $4.81

Average Price Point With Historical Data

46% of sales come from the $3.50 items

21% of sales come from the $6.00 items

33% of sales come from the $4.95 items

(($3.50*46)+($6.00*21)+($4.95*33))=

$450.35

$450.35/100 = $4.50

Weighed Average for Calculations: $4.50

Next, in order to calculate how many hours a month Drew has to work in order to breakeven on his operating costs, he needs to divide his average Monthly Estimated Expense by his average hourly rate.

$479 average monthly estimated expenses (not including start-up costs)

$42.50 average hourly rate

$479/$42.50 = $11.27

Drew must work a minimum of 11.27 hours in order to cover his operating expenses. Hours worked above and beyond that will be pre-tax profit for his company minus any direct variable costs for things like dog treats that additional services incur.

Break-even for Services Companies

_____ Average Hourly Rate

_____ Average Monthly Estimated Expenses (not including start-up costs)

Average Monthly Expenses/Average Hourly Rate = Number of Hours Required to Breakeven

_____ / _____ = _____

Products companies should follow a similar format to service providers like Drew and divide their average Monthly Estimated Expenses by the average price of their products in order to determine how many units of product need to be sold before the business will breakeven on its operating expenses.

It's worth noting two things. First, remember that any products sold over and above break-even are not pure profit. Since there are costs associated with the production of each product, product providers' profits above the break-even units of sales comes from the difference between what each unit is being sold for and how much it costs to make that unit. Secondly, this breakeven analysis is not exact since it doesn't take into account what happens when, for example, the variable costs that you've estimated for in your Monthly Estimated Expenses change dramatically. If those variable costs go up, so too will the number of products you need to sell in order to breakeven. Also, if it turns out that you only end up selling the low-priced products and not your higher-priced items then your weighted average product price would decrease and the number of units necessary to break-even would increase.

Break-even for Product Companies

_____ Average Product Price

_____ Average Monthly Estimated Expenses (not including start-up costs)

Average Monthly Expenses/Average Product Price = Number of Units Sold Required to Breakeven

_____ / _____ = _____

What If My Break-Even Is Too High?

You may find that the number of products you have to sell or the total number of hours you need to work in order to break-even is simply unrealistic either at this point in time or unrealistic in terms of fitting in with your overall life (remember that Visioning exercise?). If part of what you value is flexibility and time to spend with your family or friends, don't' get caught in a vortex of needing to work 80-hour weeks just to break-even on your operating expenses! If you find yourself in this situation after this exercise you can go back and evaluate each of the following to determine where you might be able to make changes:

1. Are your variable costs too high? Is there a way to cut your variable costs without affecting the quality of what you're offering? Obviously you don't want to cut your costs if it will negatively impact your business as you want customers to have a good experience and become repeat customers. Check to see if there might be ways to lower your variable costs or make substitutions that won't impact quality or customer experience.

2. Are your prices too low? Have you priced your products or services in such a way that you're to giving yourself enough of profit? Go back and look at your target market and at the prices your direct competitors are charging and see if your prices are in line with what the market can and will pay.

3. Are your fixed operating costs too high? You may really want to move into that beautiful window-framed storefront, but that cost may be too high for your business at this juncture. Maybe you need to think about finding a less expensive place to rent or even work out of your home (if applicable for your business model) for some time while you build your business. Take a look through all your fixed operating costs and see where you might be able to cut expenses. As you evaluate each operating cost, be sure to stay realistic. It may be tempting to dropt that business cell phone bill from $100/month to $25 but are you actually going to be able to stick to that lower plan without going over in minutes or data which may end up costing you more in the long run? Don't be tempted to fall into the trap of inputting lower expense figures just to make your break-even figures look better.

Forecasting Your Cash Inflows & Outflows

The last step in the financial part of our business plan is to add the anticipated revenue based on your Monthly Estimated Expenses worksheet so that we can try to determine approximately how much money you will be making every month. Remember when you created that Vision Statement at the beginning of this workbook? This step in the business planning process is going to help determine if the business you've designed financially matches up with the vision you have for your business. Is this business going to provide you with the financial freedom to leave that full-time job you've dreamed of leaving? Or will it give you, in addition to a creative outlet, enough financial flexibility that you feel comfortable going ahead and arranging that nanny-share? Money is not the end-all-be-all in life, but when it comes to running a business it is important to know if your hard work will provide you with the type of financial success that you're anticipating.

The good news is that you've already done most of the work necessary to create your Monthly Cash Forecast. You simply take the expenses you identified in your Monthly Estimated Expenses worksheet and input them into the correct expense lines in the Monthly Cash Forecast. You may notice that there's something missing from this worksheet though – it's just expenses! What about the revenue you anticipate making from selling your products or services? That's what we need to add in!

Projecting your sales is more art than science when you're first starting your business because you have no solid way of knowing what the demand will be for your product or service but at least you have your Breakeven calculations to fall back on. Based on your breakeven numbers, ask yourself how realistic it is that you could sell more units or hours in order to surpass your breakeven point. Do you have the distribution channels necessary to sell more? By that I mean, for services companies how do you plan to get new clients? Perhaps you already have a group of people who would like to work with you or perhaps you plan on going to networking events or advertising to bring in new clients. For product companies, do you know of certain farmers' markets or crafts fairs where you could sell your products and start to gain attention for them? Or if you're planning to sell your products online, do you plan to spend some money to help drive people to your website?

As you think about what you have planned for your business and how you anticipate reaching new customers, how many hours, for services companies, or how many products, for product companies, do you anticipate selling each month? You should multiply this number by your Average Hourly Rate or your Average Product Price and input that number into the Projected Sales line of the Monthly Cash Forecast.

Remember to be realistic! For most new small businesses, the business may not jump right out of the gate and have you working at full capacity. It may take some time to build up a customer base. If you believe this to be the case, your Projected Sales line should reflect that and show your sales growing over time. Remember though, as you work less (or more), your variable costs will also change so you want to make sure those numbers are adjusted in your worksheet as well.

This is another example of where any actual sales data you have can be very helpful. If you've already started your business and have some concrete sales numbers you can use these as a starting point as you project future months; sales revenue.

After you've input your Projected Sales for each month you can determine how much profit (or loss) your company would experience under that scenario. Subtract all of your costs from your Projected Sales and input that resulting number for each month on the Net Profit(Loss) line of the worksheet. Remember, sales don't grow in a straight line, be prepared for dips and slow periods as your business gathers momentum. (You may want to make additional copies of the next worksheet to account for a full year).

Monthly Cash Forecast

Month:

Fixed Costs							
Office/Facilities Rent							
Telephone/Internet							
Accounting Fees							
Total Fixed Costs							
(Add all fixed costs together)							
Variable Costs							
Raw Materials/Direct Product Costs							
Marketing							
Association Fees							
Print Marketing							
Online Marketing							
Website							
Payroll							
Office Supplies							
Total Variable Costs							
(Add all variable costs together)							
Other Costs							
Business Licenses							
Other Permits							
Legal fees							
Total Other Costs							
(Add all other costs together)							
Total Monthly Estimated Expenses							
(Add Total Fixed, Total Variable, and Total Other together)							
Projected Sales							
Net Profit (pre-tax)							
(Projected Sales - Total Monthly Estimated Expenses)							

Monthly Cash Forecast
(Aunt B's Jams)

Month:	Startup	April	May	June	July	Aug	Sept
Fixed Costs							
Office/Facilities Rent	$250	$250	$250	$250	$250	$250	$250
Telephone/Internet	$115	$115	$115	$115	$115	$115	$115
Accounting Fees	$30	$30	$30	$30	$30	$30	$30
Total Fixed Costs	$395	$395	$395	$395	$395	$395	$395
(Add all fixed costs together)							
Variable Costs							
Raw Materials/Direct Product Costs	$125	$125	$150	$250	$250	$300	$300
Marketing							
Association Fees	$30	$30	$30	$30	$30	$30	$30
Print Marketing	-	-	-	-	-	-	-
Online Marketing	$25	$25	$25	$25	$25	$25	$25
Website	-	-	-	-	-	-	-
Payroll	$1,500	-	-	-	-	-	-
Office Supplies	$25	$25	$25	$25	$25	$25	$25
Total Variable Costs	$1,705	$205	$230	$330	$330	$380	$380
(Add all variable costs together)							
Other Costs							
Business Licenses	$150	-	-	-	-	-	-
Other Permits	$400	-	-	-	-	-	-
Legal fees	-	-	-	-	-	-	-
Total Other Costs	$550	0	0	0	0	0	0
(Add all other costs together)							
Total Monthly Estimated Expenses	$2,650	$600	$625	$725	$725	$775	$775
(Add Total Fixed, Total Variable, and Total Other together)							
Projected Sales	0	$1,123	$1,348	$1,617	$1,617	$2,122	$2,122
Net Profit (pre-tax)	$-2,650	$523	$723	$892	$892	$1,347	$1,347
(Projected Sales - Total Monthly Estimated Expenses)							

Monthly Estimated Expenses
(Drew's Dog Walking Service)

Month:	Startup	Jan	Feb	March	April	May	June
Fixed Costs							
Office/Facilities Rent	-	-	-	-	-	-	-
Telephone/Internet	$150	$150	$150	$150	$150	$150	$150
Accounting Fees	$30	$30	$30	$30	$30	$30	$30
Total Fixed Costs	$180	$180	$180	$180	$180	$180	$180
(Add all fixed costs together)							
Variable Costs							
Raw Materials/Direct Product Costs	-	$12	$12	$40	$40	$50	$50
Marketing							
Association Fees	$30	$30	$30	$30	$30	$30	$30
Print Marketing	-	$150		$150		$150	
Online Marketing	-	$40	$40	$40	$40	$40	$40
Website	$3,000	-					
Payroll	-	-					
Office Supplies	$25	$25	$25	$25	$25	$25	$25
Total Variable Costs	$3,055	$309	$157	$335	$185	$345	$195
(Add all variable costs together)							
Other Costs							
Business Licenses	$150						
Other Permits	$400						
Legal fees	$300						
Insurance	$45	$45	$45				
Total Other Costs	$845	$532	$382	$45	$45	$45	$45
(Add all other costs together)				$560	$410	$570	$420
Total Monthly Estimated Expenses	$4,130	$532	$382	$560	$410	$570	$420
(Add Total Fixed, Total Variable, and Total Other together)							
Projected Sales	$2,122	$420	$487	$1,270	$3,040	$4,200	$6,720
Net Profit (pre-tax)	$1,347	-$112	$105	$10	$2,630	$3,630	$6,300
(Projected Sales - Total Monthly Estimated Expenses)							

As you look at your anticipated Net Profit every month, keep a close eye on those months where you experience a loss or where your profit is just barely above zero. While most new small businesses do experience months of loss before they're able to get into the black, you have to ask yourself whether you're comfortable losing that money in the short term. Depending on where you are in your life and what your other financial obligations are, you may or may not be. If you fall into the latter case, you should then see if there are ways you can revise your business model so that you can more quickly recoup your investment in the business. Alternatively, you may want to seek see financing through family, friends, or perhaps even a bank loan, in order to make sure you have enough cash to get the business started in the manner you want and enough cash reserves to weather the leaner months.

The second thing you want to evaluate as you look at the Monthly Cash Forecast is if your projected profit has you on track to meet that Vision Statement you created at the beginning of this process. Keep in mind that the profits we're projecting here are only for the first year whereas the Vision Statement was designed to capture a day in your life three years from now, but you want to feel that what you're accomplishing during the first year has you on track to achieve that three year vision for your life. Once again, if not, then you should re-evaluate your business model to try and determine what you need to change in order to get you moving in the right direction.

I realize that by this point, after all this work, the last thing you really want to do is re-evaluate your business model, but if you find yourself in that situation, it is far better to re-evaluate and make changes now versus getting part-way into the next year, having invested significantly more time by then, and then trying to change course. The whole point of the business plan is to act as a viability test and if your business plan doesn't pass the test to your satisfaction it's cheaper – both in terms of time and money – to make changes now in order to be sure that your business is getting off on the right foot.

Section Checklist

Choose Your Accounting and Financial Tools

Determine Your Cost of Goods Sold (COGS)

Price Your Products/Services Appropriately

Estimate Your Start-Up Expenses

Calculate Your Break-Even

Create Your Monthly Cash Forecasts

SECTION 4: CREATING YOUR BUSINESS ACTION PLAN

This is where most business plans and business planning books end. Now, you have completed all of the components of a business plan and hopefully the process of working through this plan has helped get your thoughts organized and kept you excited about the future in addition to pointing out areas where your business model could use revisions or improvements. But a business plan is just a bunch of paper and that's not much use to you in starting and growing your business if you don't execute on it. So let's spend a bit of time taking what you've created and turning it into an actionable plan so that you can start working towards achieving those business goals of yours immediately.

Short-term To Do List

First, this business plan is taking into account what you hope to achieve in the next year, but what about in the critical next 90 days? You've built momentum and energy working through this plan so you should leverage that immediately. There are very real tactical things you need to complete to just get your business through the next three months. If you haven't yet gotten your business licenses then that's Step 1. What about getting an email address for your business? Or perhaps you've been meaning to try and coordinate a nanny-share so that you can work on your business uninterrupted 3 days a week. These don't have to be major to-do's, but they are the beginning of removing some of those barriers that stand between you and business success. Whatever type of business you're planning and regardless of where your business is in its lifecycle, there are undoubtedly hundreds of loose ends you need to tie up. Rather than focus on a million though, what are the 10-15 most important of those loose ends that you need to complete in the next 90 days so that you can start moving your business forward. Write those to-do's down, post this somewhere you can't forget it, and then work towards getting those to-do's checked off!

Developing An Annual Action Plan

You've already devoted a lot of time and thought to your business plan. Now let's take the core of the information you put into that plan and condense it into a one-page action plan that you can refer to as you make business decisions in the next year. In fact, the following Action Plan worksheet was specifically designed so that it would be easy to keep close at hand so be sure to post it close to your computer, in your workspace, or you could even save it as your screen saver! You may want to make several blank copies of the Action Plan worksheet so that you can break your annual Action Plan down into monthly or quarterly plans if you find that would help you stay on track throughout the year.

To complete the Action Plan, start by filling in the top 3 goals you outlined back in Section 1. You want to word these so that the goals are as specific and measurable as possible. For example, one of Aunt B's goals was to increase jam sales but she had not set metrics by which she was going to measure her success. So rather than simply write 'Increase jam sales' in this action plan, she'll write 'Increase annual jam sales by 36%.'

After you've added in your goals, the next step is to outline the 2 – 3 strategies that you plan to undertake to reach those goals. In this case, strategies should be thought of as your high-level plans to help you reach those goals. For example, in order to increase her jam sales by 36% in the next year, one of Aunt B's strategies might be to provide an online shopping option for consumers in order to generate more sales.

When you think about the strategies you're going to use to help you achieve your goals, make sure you continue to learn as much as you can about your target market and the marketplace as it's always changing.

There's one last part to complete and that's the Tactics. For each strategy, you should include 2 – 3 tactics – the actual tangible things you're going to do and by when – in order to achieve those strategies and move you closer to your goal. Using that Aunt B's example again, tied to her provide an online shopping option, the related tactic would be to design and launch an online store where consumers can shop for Aunt B's products' anytime day or night.

Annual Action Plan

Goals	Strategies	Tactics
Goal 1	Strategy 1	Tactic 1
	Strategy 2	Tactic 2
Goal 2	Strategy 1	Tactic 1
	Strategy 2	Tactic 2
	Strategy 3	Tactic 3
Goal 3	Strategy 1	Tactic 1
	Strategy 2	Tactic 2
	Strategy 3	Tactic 3

Annual Action Plan
(Aunt B's Jams)

Goals	Strategies	Tactics
Increase monthly sales by 36%	Provide online shopping option	Create an online store where consumers can shop for products 24x7
	Add sales channels	Add 2 more farmers markets in order to build brand awareness
Introduce 3 new flavors	Know what the market wants	Do informal polls at farmers markets & online to see what flavors customers want
	Product launch	Create a marketing plan for the new products so new products sales increase
	Build word of mouth	Create awareness of new flavors by sampling them out at select events
Get into 5 retail locations	Build realtionships with key buyers	Identify key stores and begin to reach out to store buyers
	Make sure products sell well in stores	Develop point-of-purchase material to help increase instore sales
	Promotional strategy	Create promotions such as Buy 1, Get 1...can use to help... by new customers

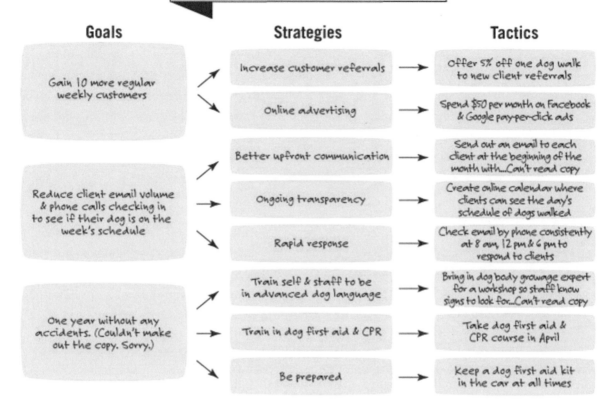

Annual Action Plan
(Drew's Dog Walking Service)

Goals	Strategies	Tactics
Gain 10 more regular weekly customers	Increase customer referrals	Offer 5% off one dog walk to new client referrals
	Online advertising	Spend $50 per month on Facebook & Google pay-per-click ads
Reduce client email volume & phone calls checking in to see if their dog is on the week's schedule	Better upfront communication	Send out an email to each client at the beginning of the month with...Can't read copy
	Ongoing transparency	Create online calendar where clients can see the day's schedule of dogs walked
	Rapid response	Check email by phone consistently at 8 am, 12 pm & 6 pm to respond to clients
One year without any accidents. (Couldn't make out the copy. Sorry.)	Train self & staff to be in advanced dog language	Bring in dog body growage expert for a workshop so staff know signs to look for...Can't read copy
	Train in dog first aid & CPR	Take dog first aid & CPR course in April
	Be prepared	Keep a dog first aid kit in the car at all times

Congratulations, a business plan is no easy task but by methodically and thoughtfully working through this workbook you've helped better position your business for success and I hope you found the process a little less daunting and a little less scary then it first seemed.   If you'll allow me, I'd like to close out this workbook by borrowing a few wise words from Former First Lady of the United States Eleanor Roosevelt and remind you that "the future belongs to those who believe in the beauty of their dreams." So dream big ... but plan wisely!

Business As Unusual

So many of us start our small businesses based on the business models that we've seen laid out in this workbook. For example, if you start a food business you sell initially through farmers' markets or you start a business resource company and utilize a website to get information to potential customers. There's nothing wrong with that but if all we do is copy the actions of those before us can we really expect to break through the clutter and become a business that stands out in consumers' minds? Sure, some of us will have better success than others due to a number of factors – some in and some out of our control – but we're simply playing in someone else' model. What does it take to be really successful?

When talking with entrepreneurs, the idea of 'paradigm shift' comes up again and again. Small retail storefronts are being undercut by the big online giants, small brands are getting pushed off of store shelves by lower-priced bigger competitors, and even independent food trucks are now seeing their fast-food competitors get behind the wheel. It's no doubt tough to be a small business but even harder when you're playing by someone else's rules.

So can we change the paradigm in a way that benefits us? I don't have an answer to this other than to say that I know it can be done as I've seen it done before. For example, one glassmaker opened up a storefront that only sells his and other locally produced crafts – none of which are sold to big box or through online retail channels. This store is incredibly successful because all these one-of-a-kind products are located in one store making it easy for customers to know where to go when they want to find unique and thoughtful gifts. Or the company that decided to start sending out a catalogue rather than trying to get a spot in someone else's catalogue. So there are ways...it's just figuring out what might be the right way for you.

As you complete this business plan and begin working through your action plan, keep your mind open for ways that you can shift the paradigm. Is there something you can change that will WOW your customers? Don't be surprised if you don't have any answers right away – it's not necessarily an easy question to answer. But sometimes I've found that by just putting the question out there and letting it percolate you may find your way to the answer.

Other Books By Jennifer Lewis

Starting A Part-Time Food Business
Everything You Need To Know To Turn Your Love For Food Into
A Successful Business Without Necessarily Quitting Your Day Job

Handmade
How Eight Everyday People Became Artisan Food Entrepreneurs And Their Recipes For Success

Getting Your Specialty Food Product Onto Store Shelves
The Ultimate Wholesale How To Guide For Artisan Food Entrepreneurs

Food On Wheels
The Complete Guide To Starting A Food Truck, Food Cart, or Other Mobile Food Business

For more information and additional resources please visit www.smallfoodbiz.com.

Made in the USA
San Bernardino, CA
01 May 2015